Alexander McLachlan

Poems and songs

Alexander McLachlan

Poems and songs

ISBN/EAN: 9783744776998

Printed in Europe, USA, Canada, Australia, Japan

Cover: Foto ©Thomas Meinert / pixelio.de

More available books at **www.hansebooks.com**

Poems and Songs.

HUNTER, ROSE & CO.,
PRINTERS AND BINDERS,
TORONTO.

POEMS AND SONGS.

BY
ALEXANDER McLACHLAN.

TORONTO:
HUNTER, ROSE AND COMPANY.
1874.

Entered according to the Act of the Parliament of Canada, in the year one thousand eight hundred and seventy-four, by HUNTER, ROSE & Co., in the office of the Minister of Agriculture.

CONTENTS.

MISCELLANEOUS POEMS.

	PAGE		PAGE
God	9	Up and be a Hero	40
Garibaldi	12	Infinite	42
Old Hannah	13	Wilson's Grave	45
The Rain it falls	14	Napoleon on St. Helena	46
May	15	Martha	48
Britannia	17	Change	50
Ah, Me!	18	The Wise Woman	53
Mystery	19	Traditions	56
Who knows?	20	The Seer	57
We're all afloat	22	The Anglo-Saxon	61
Song	23	Where'er we may wander	63
Man	24	A Song of Charity	65
The Song of the Sun	27	Catholic Mother and Child	66
Ideal	30	Awful Spirit	70
Woman	32	To a Violet	73
We live in a ricketty House	34	Stars	75
David, King of Israel	35	If you would be Master	77
Robert Burns	38	O, spread the glad Tidings	78

IDYLS OF THE DOMINION.

	PAGE		PAGE
Elora	83	The Gipsy Blood	91
The Hall of Shadows	85	The Settler's Sabbath Day	93
O! Come to the Greenwood Shade	89	A Backwoods Hero	97
		Sparking	101

	PAGE		PAGE
Neighbour John	102	Spring	133
Fire in the Woods; or the Old Settler's Story	104	Going to the Bush	135
		Old Hoss	138
The Man who rose from nothing	108	Young Hoss	141
		The Death of the Ox	144
The Pines	109	October	148
The Backwoods Philosopher	111	Indian Summer	151
Old Canada; or, Gee Buck, Gee	114	Hurrah for the New Dominion	154
Companions in Solitude; or Reminiscences of the Bush	116	Acres of your own	155
		Whip-Poor-Will	156
Young Canada; or, Jack's as good's his Master	116	Ontario	157
		The Maple Tree	159
The Old Settler's Address to his old Log-house	120	Autumn Leaves	160
		Bobolink	161
The Maple and the Thistle; or, Roderick of the Hammer	123	To an Indian's Skull	162
		Grandmother's Story to her Grand-children; or, the Evil Eye	166
The Pic-Nic	125		
To a Humming Bird	129		
"Wee Davie Lowe"	131		

MISCELLANEOUS SCOTTISH PIECES.

	PAGE		PAGE
Hallowe'en	171	The Death of Evan Dhu	198
Cartha again	176	Love	201
Scotland re-visited; or, the Wanderer's Return	177	The Lang Heided Laddie	202
		Hugh Macdonald	204
Paisley Abbey	180	Sighs in the City	208
Lord Lindsay's Return	184	When George the Fourth was King	210
Scotland	186		
The Sempill Lords	188	The Age of Jollity	212
Mary White	190	Old Adam	214
I winna gae hame	192	The Halls of Holyrood	218
The Wee Laddie's Summer Day	195	We're a' John Tamson's Bairns	220
		Longings in London	222

Miscellaneous Poems.

MISCELLANEOUS POEMS.

GOD.

HAIL, Thou great mysterious Being!
Thou the unseen, yet All-seeing,
    To Thee we call.
How can a mortal sing Thy praise,
Or speak of all Thy wondrous ways?
    God over all.

God of the great old solemn woods,
God of the desert solitudes
    And trackless sea;
God of the crowded city vast,
God of the present and the past,
    Can man know Thee?

God of the blue vault overhead,
Of the green earth on which we tread,
    Of time and space;
God of the worlds which Time conceals,
God of the worlds which Death reveals
    To all our race.

God of the glorious realms of thought,
From which some simple hearts have caught
    A ray divine;
And the songs which rouse the nations,
And the terrible orations,
    Lord God are Thine.

And all the forms of beauty rare,
Which toiling genius moulds with care,
    Yea, the sublime,
The sculptured busts of joy and woe
By Thee were fashioned long ago,
    In that far clime.

Far above earth and space and time,
Thou dwellest in Thy heights sublime.
    Beneath Thy feet
The rolling worlds, the heavens are spread,
Glory infinite round Thee shed,
    Where angels meet.

From out Thy wrath the earthquakes leap,
And shake the world's foundations deep,
    Till nature groans.
In agony the mountains call,
And ocean bellows throughout all
    Her frightened zones.

But where Thy smile its glory sheds,
The lilies lift their lovely heads,
    And the primrose rare:
And the daisy, deck'd with pearls
Richer than the proudest earls
    On their mantles wear.

These Thy preachers of the wild-wood,
Keep they not the heart of childhood
    Fresh within us still ?
Spite of all our life's sad story,
There are gleams of Thee and glory
    In the daffodil.

And old Nature's heart rejoices,
And the rivers lift their voices,
    And the sounding sea ;
And the mountains, old and hoary,
With their diadems of glory,
    Shout, Lord, to Thee !

But though thou art high and holy,
Thou dost love the poor and lowly,
    With a love divine,
Love infinite ! love supernal,
Love undying ! love eternal,
    Lord God are thine !

GARIBALDI.

SONS of Italy, awake,
Your hearths and altars are at stake
Arise, arise, for Freedom's sake,
    And strike with Garibaldi!

The Liberator now appears,
Foretold by prophets, bards, and seers,
The hero sprung from blood and tears
    All hail to Garibaldi!

Let serfs and cowards fear and quake
O Venice, Naples, Rome, awake!
Like lava of your burning lake,
    Rush on with Garibaldi!

Up and avenge your country's shame;
Like Ætna belching forth her flame,
Rush on in Freedom's holy name,
    And strike with Garibaldi!

'Tis Freedom thunders in your ears:
The weary night of blood and tears,
The sorrows of a thousand years,
    Cry "On with Garibaldi!"

The Roman Eagle is not dead
Her mighty wings again are spread
To swoop upon the tyrant's head,
    And strike with Garibaldi!

The land wherein the laurel waves
Was never meant to nourish slaves;
Then onward to your bloody graves,
    Or live like Garibaldi!

OLD HANNAH.

'TIS Sabbath morn, and a holy balm
　Drops down on the heart like dew,
　　And the sunbeams gleam
　　Like a blessed dream
　　Afar on the mountains blue.
Old Hannah's by her cottage door,
　In her faded widow's cap;
　　She is sitting alone
　　On the old grey stone,
　With the Bible in her lap.

An oak is hanging above her head,
　And the burn is wimpling by;
　　The primroses peep
　　From their sylvan keep,
　And the lark is in the sky.
Beneath that shade her children played,
　But they're all away with Death,
　　And she sits alone
　　On the old grey stone,
　To hear what the Spirit saith.

Her years are o'er three score and ten,
　And her eyes are waxing dim,
　　But the page is bright
　　With a living light,
　And her heart leaps up to Him
Who pours the mystic harmony
　Which the soul can only hear!
　　She is not alone
　　On the old grey stone,
　Tho' no earthly friend is near.

There's no one left to love her now;
But the eye that never sleeps
    Looks on her in love
    From the heavens above,
And with quiet joy she weeps;
For she feels the balm of bliss is poured
In her lone heart's deepest rut;
    And the widow lone
    On the old grey stone,
Has a peace the world knows not.

THE RAIN IT FALLS.

THE rain it falls, and the wind it blows,
And the restless ocean ebbs and flows,
But the why and the wherefore no one knows.

The races come and the races go,
But alas! alas! what do they know?
They but repeat the old tale of woe.

The years they come and they hurry on,
Ah, just as they did in the days agone!
And bear us back to the vast unknown.

We can't resist the decrees of Fate,
And there's nothing for us but to wait
'Till Death shall open or shut the gate.

For the rain may fall, and the wind may blow,
And the generations come and go,
But the why and the wherefore none may know.

MAY.

SING and rejoice!
Give to gladness a voice
Shout a welcome to beautiful May!
    Rejoice with the flowers,
    And the birds 'mong the bowers,
And away to the green woods, away!
    O, blithe as the fawn
    Let us dance in the dawn
Of this life-giving, glorious day:
    'Tis bright as the first
    Over Eden that burst—
O, welcome, young joy-giving May!

    The cataract's horn
    Has awakened the Morn,
Her tresses are dripping with dew;
    O, hush thee, and hark!
    'Tis her herald, the lark,
That's singing afar in the blue.
    Its happy heart's rushing,
    In strains wildly gushing,
That reach to the revelling earth,
    And sink through the deeps
    Of the soul, till it leaps
Into raptures far deeper than mirth.

    All nature's in keeping!
    The live streams are leaping
And laughing in gladness along;
    The great hills are heaving,

The dark clouds are leaving,
The valleys have burst into song.
   We'll range through the dells
   Of the bonnie blue bells,
And sing with the streams on their way;
   We'll lie in the shades
   Of the flower-covered glades,
And hear what the primroses say.

   O, crown me with flowers
   'Neath the green spreading bowers,
With the gems and the jewels May brings;
   In the light of her eyes
   And the depth of her dyes,
We'll smile at the purple of kings.
   We'll throw off our years
   With their sorrows and tears,
And time will not number the hours
   We'll spend in the woods,
   Where no sorrow intrudes,
With the streams and the birds and the flowers.

BRITANNIA.

ALL hail, my country! hail to thee,
Thou birthplace of the brave and free
Thou ruler upon land and sea,
     Britannia!

No thing of change, no mushroom state
In wisdom thou canst work and wait,
Or wield the thunderbolts of Fate,
     Britannia!

Oh, nobly hast thou played thy part!
What struggles of the head and heart
Have gone to make thee what thou art,
     Britannia!

Great mother of the mighty dead!
Sir Walter sang and Nelson bled
To weave a garland for thy head,
     Britannia!

And Watt, the great magician, wrought,
And Shakspeare ranged the realms of thought,
And Newton soared, and Cromwell fought,
     Britannia!

And Milton's high seraphic art,
And Bacon's head and Burns' heart
Are glories that shall ne'er depart,
     Britannia!

These are the soul of thy renown,
The gems immortal in thy crown,
The suns that never shall go down,
      Britannia!

O, still have faith in truth divine!
Aye sacred be thy seal and sign,
And power and glory shall be thine,
      Britannia!

AH, ME!

GO seek the shore and learn the lore
 Of the great old mystic sea,
And with list'ning ear you'll surely hear
 The great waves sigh, "Ah, me!"

There's a Harper good in the great old wood,
 And a mighty ode sings he;
To his harp he sings with its thousand strings,
 And the burden is, "Ah, me!"

A glorious sight are the orbs of light
 In Heaven's wide azure sea;
Yet to our cry they but reply,
 With a long deep sigh, "Ah, me!"

And Death and Time, on their march sublime,
 They will not questioned be;
And the hosts they bore to the dreamless shore
 Return no more, Ah, me!

MYSTERY.

MYSTERY! Mystery!
All is a mystery!
Mountain and valley, and woodland and stream;
Man's troubled history,
Man's mortal destiny,
Are but a phase of the soul's troubled dream.

Mystery! Mystery!
All is a mystery!
Heart throbs of anguish and joy's gentle dew
Fall from a fountain
Beyond the great mountain
Whose summits for ever are lost in the blue.

Mystery! Mystery!
All is a mystery!
The sigh of the night winds, the song of the waves,
The visions that borrow
Their brightness from sorrow,
The tales which flowers tell us, the voices of graves.

Mystery! Mystery!
All is a mystery!
Ah! there is nothing we wholly see through!
We are all weary,
The night's long and dreary—
Without hope of morning, O, what would we do?

WHO KNOWS?

THE night was dark and the winds were out,
    And the stars hid in the sky,
And the mousing owl too-hoo'd aloud
    At the wan moon rushing by ;
And there I sat in my lonely room,
    With the children all asleep ;
Ah ! there they lay in their dreams at play,
    While I sat with my sorrows deep.

I ponder'd long on this weary life,
    And I cried " Are we what we seem :
Or sail we here in a phantom ship,
    In search of a vanished dream ?
From deep to deep, from doubt to doubt,
    While the night still deeper grows ;
Who knows the meaning of this life ?"
    When a voice replied, " *Who Knows ?*"

" Shall it always be a mystery ?
    Are there none to lift the veil ?
Knows no one aught of the land we left,
    Or the port to which we sail ?
Poor shipwrecked mariners, driven about
    By every wind that blows :
Is there a haven of rest at all ?"
    And the voice replied, " *Who Knows ?*"

O, why have we longings infinite,
    And affections deep and high,
And glorious dreams of immortal things,
    If they are but born to die ?
Are they but will-o'-wisps, that gleam
    Where the deadly night-shade grows ;
Do they end in dust and ashes all ?"
    And the voice still cried, " *Who Knows ?*"

And its hopeless tones fell on my heart
    Like a dark and heavy cloud,
While the great horn'd moon looked down on me
    In terror from its shroud.
And it plainly said, "Ye are orphans all;
    Is there no balm for your woes?"
While the screech-owl cried and the night wind sighed,
    Alas! alas! "*Who Knows?*"

I prayed for light through that weary night,
    And I question'd saint and seer;
But the demon Doubt put all to rout,
    And kept ringing in mine ear
"Your life's a trance and a spectral dance,
    And round and round ye go;
Ye are poor ghosts all at a spectral ball,
    And that is the most ye know.

"Ye dance and sing in your spectral ring,
    Tho' affrighted Nature raves
Tho' the screech-owls cry and the night winds sigh,
    And the dead turn in their graves.
Ye come like thought, and ye pass to nought,
    And what is surprising most,
'Mid your ghostly fun there is hardly one
    That believes himself a ghost.

"O, thought is sad, it would make you mad;
    It is folly to weep and rave;
So follow Mirth around the earth,
    For there's nought beyond the grave.
Your hearts would sink if ye dared to think,
    So ye dance with Death at the ball;
And round ye go till the cock shall crow,
    And that is the end of all."

WE'RE ALL AFLOAT.

WE'RE all afloat in a leaky boat,
    On Time's tempestuous sea;
Death at the helm steers for his realm,
    And a motley crew are we.
Through waters wide on every side,
    Away to the sunken shoals,
He steers us o'er to the Passion's roar,
    And the heave of living souls.

We hear the splash and the heavy dash,
    And the weary, weary moan,
And only know we embarked in woe,
    And are bound for the great unknown:
Some telling tales of happy vales
    That lie beyond the gloom,
While Greed and Spite are at their fight
    For another inch of room.

And Fraud and Pride how they push aside
    The weak ones and the old,
While curses deep from the mad hearts leap
    That they've huddled in the hold.
'Tis sad to hear, 'mid the tempest drear,
    How the selfish crew go on;
How they curse and swear and snarl there,
    As dogs do o'er a bone.

Anon, as a brief but sweet relief,
    In the midst of the fighting throng,
Some poor waif starts to cheer our hearts
    With the blessed voice of song;
He sings of Peace and the heart's increase
    When Love o'er the crew shall reign;
And the rudest bear with a willing ear,
    And each heart cries out "Amen."

SONG.

I'M sad, my love—oh sing! oh sing!
    And remove this heavy pall,
For Song is the only sacred thing
    That is left us since the fall.

Ah! yes, 'tis the very breath of life,
    And the light of all our day;
It stirs the soul like the Spartan fife,
    And charms the fiends away.

For oh! ere the voice of song was heard
    The world was all ajar,
But the pitying Heavens sent the bard,
    And confusion fled afar.

And while Desolation grimly sat,
    And mumbled the mouldering bones,
At her feet sprang trees all dropping fat,
    And a soul in the very stones.

And the wild beasts of the forest came
    And lowed in the peaceful dell,
And the herds of savage men grew tame,
    Entranced by her magic spell.

And the Mountains sang "Rejoice! rejoice!"
    To the forests of the dell,
And awful Ocean heaved her voice
    In the mighty choral swell.

And Echo heard in her cave confined,
    And she would the strain prolong,
Till universal Nature joined
    In the swelling sea of song.

I'm sad, my love—oh sing! oh sing!
    And remove this heavy pall,
For Song is the only magic thing
    That is left us since the fall.

MAN.

COME forth, ye wise ones—ye who can
Decipher Nature's mystic plan—
Come sound me but the depths of man.

What am I, and whence have I come?
No answer, save a dreary hum—
Oh! why, ye wise ones, are ye dumb?

What is this house in which I dwell?
Alas! alas! there's none can tell;
O, Nature keeps her secret well!

And all I hear, and touch, and see,
Time, and creation, are to me
A marvel and a mystery!

Great Ruler of the earth and sky!
O, from my spirit's depths I cry,
Almighty Father, "What am I?"

And what is all this world I see?
Is it what it appears to be,
An awful, stern reality?

And are these men that come and go,
Or but the shades of Joy and Woe,
All flitting through this vale below?

And what is Time, with all her cares,
Her wrinkles, furrows, and grey hairs,
The hag that swallows all she bears;

The mystic where, the when and how,
The awful, everlasting now,
The funeral wreath upon my brow ?

And for what purpose am I here,
A stranger in an unknown sphere
A thing of doubt, of hope and fear;

A waif on time all tempest-toss'd,
A stranger on an unknown coast,
A weary, wand'ring, wond'ring ghost ?

Did'st Thou not, Father, shape my course
Or am I but a causeless force—
A stream that issues from no source ?

Ah, no! within myself I see
An endless realm of mystery
A great, a vast infinity :

A house of flesh, a frail abode,
Where dwell the demon and the god,
A soaring seraph and a clod—

The hall of the celestial Nine,
The filthy stye of grovelling swine.
The animal and the divine ;

Creation's puzzle! false and true,
The light and dark, the old and new.
The slave, and yet the sovereign too.

Angel and demon, Nero, Paul,
And creeping things upon the wall,
I am the brother of them all.

A part of all things! first and last,
Linked to the future and the past,
At my own soul I glare aghast.

A spark from the eternal caught,
A living, loving thing of thought,
A miracle in me is wrought!

A being that can never die,
More wonderful than earth and sky,
A terror to myself am I.

My spirit's sweep shall have no bound.
O, I shall sail the deep profound,
A terror, with a glory crown'd!

And from this dust and demon free,
All glorified, these eyes shall see
The All in All eternally.

THE SONG OF THE SUN.

WHO'LL sing the song of the starry throng,
   The song of the Sun and Sky?
The angels bright on their thrones of light,
   Not a mortal such as I.
How vast, how deep, how infinite!
   Are the wonders spread abroad
On the outward walls of the azure halls
   Of the city of our God.

Men seldom look on the marvellous book
   Which God writes on the sky,
But they cry for food as the only good,
   Like the beasts which eat and die.
Awake! and gaze on the glorious maze!
   For every day and night,
God paints on air those pictures rare,
   To thrill us with delight.

O, come with me! O, let us flee
   Across the dewy lawn,
And see unrolled in realms of gold
   The glories of the dawn.
Behold she streaks the mountain peaks
   With the faintest tinge of gray,
But the glory hies, and the mists arise,
   And the shadows flee away.

The stars rush back from the conqueror's track,
   And the night away is driven.

While the King of Day mounts on his way
    Through the golden gates of Heaven,
And his heralds fly athwart the sky
    With a lovely rainbow hue,
Or hang around the deeps profound
    The unfathomed gulfs of blue.

The great vault reels 'neath his chariot wheels,
    And the thunder-clouds are riven,
'Til they expire in crimson fire
    On the burning floor of Heaven.
And then, O then! every hill and glen,
    Every peak and mountain old,
With a diadem of glory swims
    In a living sea of gold.

With his gorgeous train, through the blue domain
    He rushes on and on,
'Til with a round of glory crowned
    He mounts his noonday throne.
Then his burning beams with their golden gleams,
    He scatters in showers abroad,
'Til we cannot gaze on the glorious blaze
    Of the garments of the god.

Then from his throne, with an azure zone,
    The conqueror descends,
And in robes of white, through realms of light,
    His downward course he bends.
'Mid great white domes, like the happy homes
    Of the ransomed souls at rest,
Whose work is done, whose crowns are won,
    And they dwell among the blest.

How calm, how still, how beautiful !
    The very soul of peace
Seems breathing there her secret prayer
    That strife and sin may cease.
Then in the west he sinks to rest
    Far down in his ocean bed;
And he disappears, amid evening's tears,
    With a halo on his head.

But I cannot write of the marvellous sight
    At his setting last I saw ;
I can only feel, I can only kneel,
    With a trembling fearing and awe.
Who'll sing the song of the starry throng,
    The song of the Sun and Sky ?
The angels bright on their thrones of light,
    Not a mortal such as I.

IDEAL.

I'M lord of a realm ideal,
    And I love to steal away
From all the things which fret us here
    In this weary house of clay.
When all my sins and follies
    In judgment 'gainst me rise,
And I dare not seek a refuge
    In the common court of lies.
When I'm weary of all this world,
    When the woe will not depart,
I flee to the living streams that sing
    Through those regions of the heart.

When I hear some ancient ballad,
    Some old-world weary air,
On the wings of that old melody,
    In a moment I am there.
Away in the realms transcendent,
    Where all lovely forms have birth,
And the glorious things we see in dreams,
    But never can find on earth.
Where the flowers are always blooming,
    And the streams are never dry,
Where friendship knows no blighting,
    And our dear ones never die.

Where hope keeps all her promises,
    And there's no one sighs " Ah me,"
O'er glorious things which might have been,
    But were destined not to be.

Where worth is always welcome,
　　Where no Homer begs his bread,
Where no Kossuth is in exile,
　　With a price upon his head.
Where no son of song or of science,
　　Is scorned by the fools he'd save;
Where no great heart, in its misery,
　　Creeps into a nameless grave.

And there I meet with the humble souls,
　　That on earth bore a heavy load;
Yet soared sublime o'er the woes of time,
　　By implicit faith in God.
I meet with the mighty spirits
　　Who righted humanity's wrongs,
And the Hebrew bards and prophets,
　　Who sung the immortal songs.
I talk with the orators of old,
　　And, in listening to their tones,
I feel how they thrilled the souls of men,
　　And roused up the very stones.

With the old world's hoary sages,
　　I have converse deep and high,
While we drink the immortal nectar,
　　From founts that are never dry.
And we pledge the young immortals
　　Of every creed and clime,
Who toil below, amid want and woe,
　　To hasten earth's happy time.
And we sing the songs supernal,
　　And we shout for joy to see
Things not as we find them here on earth,
　　But things as they ought to be.

WOMAN.

WHEN my gloomy hour comes on me,
    And I shun the face of man,
Finding bitterness in all things,
    As vex'd spirits only can :

When of all the world I'm weary,
    Then some gentle woman's face,
Coming like a blessed vision,
    Reconciles me to our race.

All the children of affliction,
    All the weary and oppress'd,
Flee to thee, beloved woman,
    Finding shelter in thy breast.

While we follow mad ambition,
    Thine is far the nobler part ;
Nursing flowers of sweet affection
    In the valleys of the heart.

Man can look and laugh at danger,
    Mighty with the sword is he ;
But he cannot love, and suffer,
    Pity, and forgive, like thee.

Blessed ministers of mercy !
    Hov'ring round the dying bed,
Come to cheer the broken-hearted,
    To support the drooping head.

Oh, my blessings be upon you,
    For, beneath yon weary sky,
Ye are ever bringing comfort
    Unto sinners such as I.

When the saints have but upbraidings
    For the guilty, erring man,
Ye speak words of hope and mercy,
    As dear woman only can.

When my weary journey's ending;
    When my troubl'd spirit flies,
May a woman smooth my pillow,
    May a woman close my eyes.

WE LIVE IN A RICKETY HOUSE.

WE live in a rickety house,
    In a dirty dismal street,
Where the naked hide from day,
    And thieves and drunkards meet.

And pious folks, with their tracts,
    When our dens they enter in,
They point to our shirtless backs,
    As the fruits of beer and gin.

And they quote us texts, to prove
    That our hearts are hard as stone;
And they feed us with the fact,
    That the fault is all our own.

And the parson comes and prays—
    He's very concerned 'bout our souls;
But he never asks, in the coldest days,
    How we may be off for coals.

It will be long ere the poor
    Will learn their grog to shun;
While it's raiment, food and fire,
    And religion all in one.

I wonder some pious folks
    Can look us straight in the face,
For our ignorance and crime
    Are the Church's shame and disgrace.

We live in a rickety house,
    In a dirty dismal street,
Where the naked hide from day,
    And thieves and drunkards meet.

DAVID, KING OF ISRAEL.

COME and look upon this picture,
    Thoughtfully those features scan,
There he sits, the bard of Scripture,
    Not an angel, but a man.

In his hand, the harp that often
    Thrilled the shepherd in the glen,
And has now supreme dominion
    O'er the hearts and souls of men.

That same harp which charmed the demon
    In the darkened soul of Saul;
And has soothed the troubled spirit
    In the bosoms of us all.

Human nature's strength and weakness,
    Hope and heart-break, smiles and sighs;
What a world of joy and sorrows
    Mirrored in those deep blue eyes.

'Tis a face that, somehow, tells us
    God has made us all the same,
Of one blood, and heart and nature,
    Differing but in creed and name.

All that has been done or suffer'd,
    All that has been thought or said,
Israel's strength, and Israel's weakness,
    Summed up in that lordly head.

Yet, curtail'd, hemm'd in and hamper'd,
    He could only utter part
Of the great infinite message,
    That was lying on his heart.

'Tis a face supremely human,
   Brother to us, every one,
For he oft has sinned and sorrowed,
   Just as you and I have done.

Yes, it tells a tale of struggle,
   Of a life-long weary fight,
Wrestling with foes all the day long,
   And with phantoms all the night.

Fighting with infatuation;
   Scorning the degrading chain;
Hating sin, yet rushing to it,
   Rising but to fall again.

Always sinning and repenting,
   Promising to sin no more;
Now resisting, now consenting,
   Human to the very core.

Now he deems himself forsaken,
   Feels that he's a poor outcast;
But tho' he should die despairing,
   He will struggle to the last.

He has felt the soul's upbraiding;
   Conscience oft has made him smart,
Until pain, and shame, and sorrow
   Leapt in lyrics from his heart.

From the depth of his affliction,
   To the Father he would cry,
Who, in love and pity, raised him,
   Set him on a rock on high.

Gave him gleams of worlds transcendent,
   Brighter than the rainbow's rim;
Touched his harpstrings with the raptures
   Of the soaring seraphim.

Like the mighty waters gushing,
  Is the torrent of his song;
Sweeping onward, roaring, rushing,
  Bearing human hearts along.

Then anon, like gentle dew-drops,
  Falls that spirit—sweet, serene,
Peaceful as the quiet waters,
  Fragrant as the glades of green.

Then what living gusts of gladness
  Startle the enraptured ear,
While a tone of human sadness
  Makes the sweetest strain more dear.

Not the rapt and holy prophet,
  Not the pure in every part,
But the sinning, sorrowing creature,
  Was the "Man of God's own heart."

O, 'twas love surpassing tender,
  And God gave it as a sign,
That the heart that is most human,
  Is the heart that's most divine.

ROBERT BURNS.

Hail to thee, King of Scottish song,
    With all thy faults we 'love thee,
Nor would we set up modern saints
    For all their cant, above thee.
There hangs a grandeur and a gloom
    Around thy wondrous story,
As of the sun eclipsed at noon,
    'Mid all his beams of glory.

A marvel, and a mystery !
    A king set on a throne,
To guide the people's steps aright,
    Yet cannot guide his own.
A marvel, and a mystery !
    A strange, a wondrous birth;
Since Israel's king there has not been
    Thy likeness upon earth.

For thou wert the ordained of Heaven,
    Thy mission's high and holy;
To thee, the noble work was given,
    To lift the poor and lowly.
Thy words are living vocal things,
    Around the world they're ringing;
Hope's smiles, they bear, and everywhere
    Set weary hearts a singing.

Untutor'd child of nature wild,
    Whose instinct's always true ;
O, when I'm weary of the saints,
    I turn with joy to you.

The bigot and the blockhead still
   Are at thy memory railing,
Because thou wert a son of Eve,
   And had a human failing.

A benefactor of our race,
   Yet on the face they strike thee;
And like the Pharisee of old,
   Thank God they are not like thee.
Well, let them rave above thy grave,
   Thou canst not hear their railings:
We take thee to our heart of hearts,
   With all thy faults and failings.

For they were human at the worst
   True hearts can but deplore them;
The faults from which great virtues spring,
   O, throw a mantle o'er them!
And loving souls in every place,
   Still hail thee as a brother;
Like thee, thou glory of our race,
   Where shall we find another?

UP AND BE A HERO.

UP my friend, be bold and true,
There is noble work to do,
Hear the voice which calls on you,
      "Up, and be a hero!"

What, tho' fate has fixed thy lot,
To the lowly russet cot;
Tho' thou art not worth a *groat*,
      Thou mayest be a hero!

High heroic deeds are done,
Many a battle's lost or won,
Without either sword or gun,
      Up, and be a hero!

Not to gain a worldly height,
Not for sensual delight,
But for very love of right,
      Up, and be a hero!

Follow not the worldling's creed,
Be an honest man indeed,
God will help thee in thy need,
      Only be a hero!

There is seed which must be sown,
Mighty truths to be made known,
Tyrannies to be o'erthrown,
      Up, and be a hero!

There are hatreds and suspicions,
There are social inquisitions,
Worse than ancient superstitions,
        Strike them like a hero !

In the mighty fields of thought,
There are battles to be fought,
Revolutions to be wrought,
        Up, and be a hero !

Bloodless battles to be gained,
Spirits to be disenchained,
Holy heights to be attained.
        Up, and be a hero !

To the noble soul alone,
Nature's mystic art is shown,
God will make His secrets known,
        Only to the hero !

If thou only art but true,
What may not thy spirit do,
All is possible to you,
        Only be a hero !

INFINITE.

PART I.

UNBAR the gates of eye and ear,
Lo, what a wondrous world is here,
Marvels on marvels still appear
                    Infinite!

Great mother! by whose breast we're fed,
With thy green mantle round thee spread,
The blue vault hanging o'er thy head,
                    Infinite!

Why wert thou into being brought?
How were thy forms of beauty wrought?
Thou great upheaval of a thought,
                    Infinite!

Which scooped the vales where dew distils,
Which led the courses of the rills,
And fixed the everlasting hills,
                    Infinite!

Which called from darkness bright-eyed day,
Baptized it with a heavenly ray,
And sent it on its endless way,
                    Infinite!

Ye waves that lash the hoary steep,
Ye mighty winds with boundless sweep,
Great coursers of the trackless deep,
                    Infinite!

And you, ye streamlets on your way,
Tho' laughing all the summer's day,
Ye only sing, ye only say
                    Infinite!

Sweet linnet singing on the lea,
Wild lark in heaven's wide azure sea,
The burden of your strain's to me,
                              Infinite

Loved violets 'neath my feet that lie,
Sweet harebells, can you tell me why
Your beauty only makes me sigh?
                              Infinite!

Thou wild rose blooming on the tree,
Ye daisies laughing on the lee,
Sweet flowers your message is to me,
                              Infinite!

This dust's to spirit strangely wed,
'Tis haunted ground on which we tread,
The living, stranger than the dead,
                              Infinite!

A presence fills the earth and air,
Bends o'er us when we're not aware,
And eyes look on us everywhere,
                              Infinite

Earth, ocean, air, heaven's azure sea!
Oh, ye have always been to me
A marvel and a mystery!
                              Infinite!

PART II.

UNBAR the gates of eye and ear,
Lo! what a mystic world is here,
The heights of hope, the depths of fear,
                              Infinite!

Ye wise ones, can ye tell me nought
About this magic web of thought,
Or of the loom on which 'tis wrought?
                              Infinite!

Ye strange, ye sacred human ties,
A mighty marvel in you lies,
A wondrous world of tears and sighs,
      Infinite!

This human love, so deep, so vast;
Ye sympathies which run so fast,
And bind the future with the past,
      Infinite!

Ye magic cords, where were ye spun?
Ye strange affinities that run,
And warp the mystic web in one,
      Infinite!

Love's sacred fires, Grief's burning tears,
Faith's holy hope, and Doubt's dark fears,
Spring from a fount beyond the spheres,
      Infinite!

But, who the secret clue can find
Of all the avenues which wind
Up to thy throne, immortal mind?
      Infinite!

In the soul's presence who are great?
The wisest ones can but translate
Some passing look, some word of Fate,
      Infinite!

Who'll take the measure, or the bound?
No line of ours can ever sound
The fathomless, the great profound,
      Infinite!

O, were I but from self set free!
The spirit then might speak through me,
Of all this deep unfathomed sea,
      Infinite!

WILSON'S GRAVE.

[ALEXANDER WILSON, the Scottish Poet and American Ornithologist, is buried in the Cemetery of the Swedish Church, Southwark, Philadelphia. The Navy-yard refreshment-rooms and a wharf are within a hundred yards of his grave. "Had I been at home when he died," said his friend George Ord, " I would have selected some quiet spot in the country, retired from the city, where the birds would have warbled over his grave. Such a spot as he himself would have preferred."]

THEY should not have buried thee here !
   O ! they should have made thee a bed,
Where the flowers at thy feet would appear,
   And the birds would sing over thy head.

O ! They should have laid thee to rest,
   From the smoke of the city, away
Where the dew would fall bright on thy breast,
   And the green turf would cover thy clay.

Afar in the forest's green shade,
   The tall pine above thee should wave,
Where the "Blue-bird" would perch o'er thy head,
   And the "Whip-poor-Will" sit on thy grave.

Where Spring would come forth with her smiles,
   And the birds that to thee were so dear;
And sing 'mong the green leafy aisles,
   The songs you delighted to hear.

And the red man would marvel to meet
   A grave in the green forest shade ;
And the hunter at evening would sit,
   And weep where thine ashes are laid.

They should not have buried thee here,
   For the forest above thee should wave,
But have borne thee away on thy bier,
   Where the birds would sing over thy grave.

NAPOLEON ON ST. HELENA.

He stands alone on a desolate rock,
    With the watery waste around him;
For the slaves of Fate and the hounds of Hate,
    To this lonely rock have bound him.

No sail appears on the watery way,
    He sees but the sea-mew flying;
He hears but the wave, as it moans round this grave,
    And hope in his heart is dying.

He has folded his arms upon his breast,
    His eye's on the sun descending,
With dark clouds o'ercast, it is sinking at last,
    Like his glory in darkness ending.

And he thinks of the Sun of Austerlitz,
    That rose, and that set in glory;
And there gleams out a brief lonely joy 'mid his grief,
    For his name shall live in story.

And over that brow that was so serene,
    Tho' the death shower was descending,
A dark cloud has past, for like that sun at last,
    His glory is gloomily ending.

The sword of Marengo must rust in its sheath,
    And that soul of ambition unbounded
Must fret itself here, on this peak lone and drear:
    This rock with the ocean surrounded.

And he mutters, " Of kingdoms and crowns,
    A terrible fate has bereft me ;
They have vanished like smoke, and to rule on this rock,
    Not even that boon has been left me.

" Ah ! where are the voices that shouted so loud,
    In the day of mine exaltation ;
I hear but the moan of old ocean alone,
    Round the rock of my desolation.

" And where are the legions that leaped at my word ?
    In joy, 'mid the lightning and thunder,
While thrones shook with dread, at the sound of my tread,
    And nations stood dumb in their wonder.

" Ah, Ney ! is it thou, and Lannes and Desaix,
    With your legions, ye gather round me ?
Ye have come o'er the waves from your lone bloody graves,
    To this rock where the sea-gods have bound me.

" Let the bugles ring out ! let the eagles advance !
    There shall be no rock, and no main ;
Leap into the saddle ! great hearts, ye are able
    To bear me to glory again !

" See, Murat has broken the red gleaming ranks,
    And Junot is swooping down after ;
Ah, fool ! all my hosts turn to legions of ghosts,
    And fade amid fiendish laughter.

" I founded my kingdom on force and fraud ;
    I built on a sandy foundation ;
O ! the love-founded throne, that of Jesus alone,
    Shall smile at the waves of mutation."

MARTHA.

IN a sweet secluded nook,
Down beside the quiet brook,
There an humble cabin's seen
Peeping from the ivy green,
While a great elm bends above it,
As it really seemed to love it.
There old Martha lives alone,
But tho' to the world unknown,
There's a heart so truly human
In the breast of that old woman :
Oft I seek that quiet place,
Just to look upon her face,
And forget this scene of care,
Where men palter, curse and swear;
And the demons all are rife
In the never-ending strife
For the vanities of life.

What a world of love there lies
Mirrored in her deep blue eyes :
What a ray of quiet beauty
They throw around each daily duty :
How it is I cannot tell,
Yet I feel the magic spell
Of the quiet Sabbath grace,
Always breathing from her face,
And her voice so calm and clear
Lifts me to a higher sphere,
And unlocks my spirit's powers,
Gentle thoughts spring up like flowers.
Gems deep hidden in my heart

Into life and being start
When that saintly face I see,
Heaven and immortality
They grow clearer unto me.
She's acquaint with sin and sorrow,
Knows their weary burdens thorough,
And her hearth is the retreat
Of sad hearts, and weary feet;
And while others find but flaws,
Quoting still the moral laws,
She but thinks of what is human,
Loves them all, the dear old woman:
Time, which makes most heads but hoary,
Changed hers to a crown of glory.
Many—ah! many a benediction
From the children of affliction,—
Blessings from the haunts of care
Nestle mid the glory there;
And she always seems to me
An embodied prophesy
Of a better world to be.

CHANGE.

OH! how wondrous are the changes
    Every day and hour we see;
Things to make us ask in wonder,
    "Wherefore? and oh what are we?"
Things more wonderful than fiction,
    Or the poet's wildest dreams;
Things enough to make us question
    If this world is what it seems.
        Change! change! surpassing strange!
          What fearful changes come!
        The stars grow pale, the prophets fail,
          The oracles are dumb.

Men come forth in strength rejoicing,
    And they bid the world take note
Of their comings and their goings,
    And the mighty works they've wrought;
Deeming that they are immortal,
    How like gods they walk the scene.
Time looks in, and lo! they vanish—
    Rubb'd out as they ne'er had been.
        Change! change! surpassing strange!
          Their pomp, their power, and glory
          Are all forgot: were, and are not—
          The old eternal story.

Nations spring as 'twere from nothing,
    And are mighty in their day—
But to wax, and wane, and crumble,
    And to nothing pass away.

Great Niagara with his thunders,
  And the towering Alps sublime;
Earth and sky with all their wonders,
  Bubbles on the flood of time.
      Change! change! surpassing strange!
        Can such things surely be;
      All hurried past, and lost at last
        In Death's eternal sea?

Oh! Creation's but a vision
  Seen by the reflective eye;
But a panoramic pageant
  Pictur'd on the evening sky.
There is nothing here abiding—
  There is nothing what it seems;
Airy all, and unsubstantial,
  Wavering in a world of dreams.
      Change! change! surpassing strange!
        Is time's eternal chorus;
      We hardly know the road we go,
        Or the heavens bending o'er us.

Shall we give ourselves to pleasure?
  Drench with wine the brow of care?
That were but the coward's refuge,
  But a hiding from despair.
Shall we wed us to Ambition,
  Love, or Fame's alluring round?
Ah, alas! its promised glories
  End but in a grassy mound.
      Change! change! surpassing strange!
        There's nothing sure but sorrow;
      And we must bear our load of care,
        Nor dream of rest to-morrow.

Shall we put our trust in knowledge
  Men have garner'd here below?
Ah! the fruit of all their labour's
  But a heritage of woe.
Oh! the sum of all the knowledge,
  Garner'd underneath the sky,
Is that we are born to suffer,
  Is that we are born to die.
      Change! change! surpassing strange!
        Our knowledge comes to naught;
      And we are fooled and over-ruled
        By the very things we sought.

THE WISE WOMAN.

DRAW near, think not my tale absurd,
    For truth is strange, I ween;
I'll tell thee what mine ears have heard,
    And what mine eyes have seen.
From childhood I was void of faith
    In visions, dreams and seers;
The Spirit-World was all a myth,
    Begot of hopes and fears.

But wandering through the vale of Doubt,
    While all its gloom I felt,
At last I sought the cottage out,
    Where the wise woman dwelt.
"This is the place at last," I said,
    " Where foolish people go;
But of the unreturning dead
    What can the Sibyl know?

"The future black is all a track
    Of darkness and of doubt;
No ghost has ever yet come back
    To let the secret out.
We're travellers in a desert lone,
    And only this we know—
We issue from the Great Unknown,
    And back to it we go.

" From mystery to mystery,
    The fools of Hope and Doubt,

"We weave our little history,
   And then Death rubs us out;
And, reft of our identity,
   We can have no hereafter."
I paused in fear, for I could hear
   Sounds as of smothered laughter.

And, plainly as you hear me now,
   A voice pronounced my name,
Told me my thoughts, and why, and how
   I to the woman came;
And there she sat as still as death,
   For in a trance was she;
And yet I felt a living breath,
   Warm, breathing upon me.

And while along my veins it stole,
   And I was lost in wonder,
A light burst in upon my soul,
   A veil was rent asunder,
And there were knockings on the walls,
   And whispers long and low,
And shadows, as through empty halls,
   Were wav'ring to and fro.

And I was touched by hands unseen,
   When there was no one near;
While secrets of the dead, I ween,
   Were whispered in mine ear.
And all at once—I knew not how—
   A heavenly calm came o'er me;
When, with a glory on its brow,
   A spirit stood before me.

More beautiful it seemed to me
    Than any of earth's sons,
And clothed in all the majesty
    Of the immortal ones.
That being—once of mortal breath,
    But now a soul sublime—
Stood there, the victor over Death
    And all the shocks of Time.

The Herald of th' Eternal One!
    In mercy sent to me,
Demonstrating beneath the sun,
    Man's immortality.
And, lo! it spake: "*Ye mortals make*
    Your own Heaven or your Hell ;
Not by your creeds, but by your deeds,
    Shall ye be judged. Farewell."

When I essayed to question it
    Of glories "over there,"
Lo, it was gone! and, all alone,
    I talked to empty air.
But still that spirit holds control,
    Still watches over me,
For ever singing in my soul,
    Of glories yet to be.

TRADITIONS.

HURRAH! for the great Diana,
 And whatsoe'er ye do,
Be sure to prop the old up,
 And sacrifice the new.

Ye lean upon old traditions,
 To question them's a sin,
And stifle the holiest promptings
 Of the God that speaks within.

Ye clog the soul of Nature
 With your wretched little creeds;
Then hold up your hands in wonder,
 At the dearth of noble deeds.

Ye pray for the gods to guide you,
 Yet, when the God appears,
Ye'll have no gods but the old ones,
 And pierce His side with spears.

Ye boast of your achievements,
 Your feats with the tongue and pen,
'Til the gods look down in wonder
 At the little sons of men.

Hurrah! for the great Diana,
 And whatsoe'er ye do,
Be sure to prop the old up,
 And sacrifice the new.

THE SEER.

THE temple was a ruined heap,
  With moss and weeds o'ergrown,
And there the old Seer stood entranced,
  Beside the altar stone;
Time's broken hour-glass at his feet,
  In mouldering fragments lay;
And tombstones, whose old epitaphs
  Were eaten all away.

He pointed ever and anon,
  His eye fixed upon air,
While thus he talked to shadowy forms,
  Which seemed to hover there.

" On, on, to the regions lone,
  The generations go;
They march along to the mingled song
  Of hope, of joy, and woe.
On, on, to the regions lone,
  For there's no tarrying here,
And the hoary past is joined at last,
  By all it held so dear.

" There, there, on the edge of air,
  How fleetly they do pass,
I see them all, both great and small,
  Like pictures in a glass.
Long, long, is the motley throng,
  Of every creed and clime,
With the hopes and fears, the smiles and tears,
  Of the young and the olden time.

"Round, round, on their earthly mound,
　　The laden ages reel,
　No creak, no sound, to the ceaseless round,
　　Of Time's eternal wheel.

"There, there, with their long grey hair,
　　Are the patriarchs of our race;
A glory's shed on each hoary head,
　　As they pass with solemn pace;
Earth, earth, there were men of worth,
　　When they were in their prime,
There was less of art, and more of heart,
　　In that happy golden time.

"There, there, are the ladies fair,
　　That danced in the lordly hall;
And the minstrel grey, whose simple lay
　　Was a joy to one and all.
Fleet, fleet, were your fairy feet,
　　And ye knew the joy of tears,
While the minstrel wove the tale of love,
　　With its hopes, its doubts, and fears.

"There, there, still fresh and fair,
　　I see them march along,
The bowmen good, in the gay green wood.
　　And I hear their jocund song.
See, see, how the green oak tree,
　　With shouts they circle in,
And the stakes are set, and the champions met,
　　And the merry games begin.

　"Round, round, on their earthly mound,
　　　The laden ages reel,
　　No creak, no sound, to the ceaseless round,
　　　Of Time's eternal wheel.

" Hold, hold! Ye were barons bold,
    I know by the garb ye wear,
The lofty head, and the steady tread,
    And the trusty blades ye bear;
Where, where, are your mansions rare,
    And the lordly halls ye built;
Gone, gone, and how little's known
    Of your glory or your guilt.

" Away, away, as if to the fray,
    Ah, there they madly rush,
And in their path of woe and wrath,
    There's a dark deep purple blush:
Here, here, like the autumn sere,
    The hoary Palmers come,
Their tales they tell, of what befell,
    And the listening groups are dumb.

    " Round, round, on their earthly mound,
        The laden ages reel,
    No creak, no sound, to the ceaseless round
        Of Time's eternal wheel.

" Lo! Lo! what a splendid woe,
    Yon rearward host reveals,
It marches there with its golden care,
    To the sound of steam and wheels:
Speed, speed, oh, Guile and Greed,
    Are surely a monstrous birth,
Let wan Despair weave fabrics rare,
    And gold be the god of earth.

" Oh! oh! what a sigh of woe,
    Is from its bosom rolled,
What faces peer like winter drear,
    'Mid the glitter and the gold.

Still, still, amid all this ill,
   There are souls with a touch sublime,
Who nobly strive to keep alive,
   The hope of a happier time.

    " Round, round, on their earthly mound,
      The laden ages reel,
    No creak, no sound, to the ceaseless round,
      Of Time's eternal wheel.

" Hail! hail! to those shadows pale,
   For they were the men of thought ;
And the crags were steep, and the mines were deep,
   Where painfully they wrought ;
Speak ! speak ! why the secret keep ?
   This mystery I would know.
Say, what is breath, and life and death,
   And whither do we go ?

" Still, still, not a word ye will
   Vouchsafe to my greedy ear,
The crags are steep, and the mines are deep,
   And I can only hear :
On, on, every age has gone,
   With its burden on its back,
And spite our will with our good and ill,
   We follow in the track.

    " Round, round, on their earthly mound,
      The laden ages reel,
    No creak, no sound, to the ceaseless round,
      Of Time's eternal wheel."

THE ANGLO-SAXON.

THE Anglo-Saxon leads the van,
    And never lags behind,
For was not he ordained to be
    The leader of mankind ?
He carries very little sail,
    Makes very little show,
But gains the haven without fail,
    Whatever winds may blow.

He runs his plough in every land,
    He sails on every sea,
All prospers where he has a hand,
    For king of men is he.
He plants himself on Afric's sand,
    And 'mong Spitzbergen's snows,
For he takes root in any land,
    And blossoms like the rose.

Into the wilderness he goes,
    He loves the wild and free,
The forests stagger 'neath his blows,
    A sturdy man is he.
To have a homestead of his own,
    The giants down he'll bring—
His shanty's sacred as a throne,
    And there he'll reign a king.

For let him plant him where he may,
    On this you may depend,
As sure as worth will have the sway,
    He's ruler in the end.

For he believes in thrift, and knows
    The money-making art,
But tho' in riches great he grows,
    They harden not his heart.

He never knows when he is beat;
    To knock him down is vain,
He's sure to get upon his feet,
    And into it again.
If you're resolved to be his foe,
    You'll find him rather tough,
But he'll not strike another blow
    Whene'er you call " enough."

His is a nature true as steel,
    Where many virtues blend,
A head to think, a heart to feel,
    A soul to comprehend.
I love to look upon his face,
    Whate'er be his degree,
An honour to the human race,
    The king of men is he.

WHERE'ER WE MAY WANDER.

WHERE'ER we may wander,
 Whate'er be our lot,
The heart's first affections,
 Still cling to the spot,
Where first a fond mother,
 With rapture has prest,
Or sung us to slumber,
 In peace on her breast.

Where love first allured us,
 And fondly we hung
On the magical music,
 Which fell from her tongue!
Tho' wise ones may tell us,
 'Twas foolish and vain,
Yet, when shall we drink of
 Such glory again.

Where hope first beguiled us,
 And spells o'er us cast,
And told us her visions,
 Of beauty would last;
That earth was an Eden,
 Untainted with guile,
And men were not destined
 To sorrow and toil.

Where friendship first found us,
 And gave us her hand,
And linked us for aye, to
 That beautiful band.

Oh, still shall this heart be,
   And cold as the clay,
Ere one of their features,
   Shall from it decay.

O fortune, thy favours
   Are empty and vain ;
Restore me the friends of
   My boyhood again ;
The hearts that are scattered,
   Or cold in the tomb,
O give me again, in
   Their beauty and bloom.

Away with ambition,
   It brought me but pain,
O give me the big heart
   Of boyhood again ;
The faith and the friendship,
   The rapture of yore,
O shall they re-visit
   This bosom no more.

A SONG OF CHARITY.

COME, sing a song of Charity,
 O may she ne'er forsake us!
For good or bad, we're all what God
 And circumstances make us.
What's clear to me, is dim to thee,
 Opinions are divided;
'Tis hard to judge what's wholly fudge,
 For things are many-sided.

I hae a few thoughts o' mine ain,
 Wi nae ane would I niffer,
On sich points baith may be mistean,
 So let's agree to differ,
And sing a song of Charity,
 And may she ne'er forsake us,
For good or bad, we're all what God
 And circumstances make us.

Yet men will sigh, and wonder why
 The bigot's hither sent,
Such solemn fools are but the tools
 To work out God's intent.
O may we never do them wrong,
 Such, still, has been our prayer,
For had our lot been their's, I wot
 We'd just been such as they are.

But tho' so mad, the wars we've had—
 When Death shall send us thither—
For all that's past, we hope at last
 To meet in light together.
Then sing a song of Charity,
 And pray for truth to aid us;
For good or bad, we're all what God
 And circumstances made us.

CATHOLIC MOTHER AND CHILD.

> "O wad some Power the giftie gie us,
> To see ourselves as ithers see us."
> —Burns.

CHILD.

YOU tell me, mother, of God's grace,
    Which doth so freely flow,
But, will it ever reach the place
Where Protestants do go?

MOTHER.

No doubt they're a rebellious race,
    And hard for God to bear;
And yet, I hope, redeeming grace
    May reach them even there:
For God may not be quite so hard
    As pious Fathers say;
And Christ, for them, may speak a word
    Before the judgment day.

CHILD.

But are they not wilfully blind
    To what is plain to see?
I cannot comprehend what kind
    Of people they can be.

MOTHER.

My child, if God with them can bear,
    Then why should we condemn?
There may be some good people there,
    Yes, even among them.

Like us, no doubt, they hope and fear,
　And feel the power of love;
And shed for human woe a tear,
　And pray to God above.

CHILD.

If good, why hold they us in spite
　So terrible and strong?
It's all because we're in the right,
　And they are in the wrong.

MOTHER.

But they may think that they are right,
　And I am told they say
They have the true and only light,
　And we are all astray.

CHILD.

But they might know that is not so,
　Would they but choose to see;
They will not hear with willing ear,
　What wretches they must be!

MOTHER.

I cannot from myself conceal
　The bad course they pursue,
But sometimes they must think and feel
　The very way we do.
Sometimes I think, if they are good—
　Tho' they may not repent,
That God may—as I'm sure I would!—
　Have mercy and relent.

CHILD.

But ah, they must be wicked, who
    Would scorn the Virgin so;
Why can't they do as others do,
    And to the altar go?

MOTHER.

No doubt, my child, they put to shame
    The Saviour every day;
But 'tis their priests that are to blame,
    For leading them astray.

CHILD.

But our priests say, they take delight
    In wicked things they do;
And they would even think it right
    To murder Pa and you.

MOTHER.

It may be so, I do not know,
    I hope it is not true;
Despite the priest, I hope at least
    They know not what they do.
I often hope it can't be true,—
    As pious Fathers tell—
Their little ones, just such as you,
    God foreordain'd to Hell!
He may not spare old ones who have
    In wickedness increased;
But O, I think he'll surely save
    The little babes at least.

CHILD.

Well, good or bad, I'm very glad
    They live across the sea ;
I hope and pray they never may
    Come nearer unto me.

MOTHER.

Ah no my child ! that is not right !
    Our duty is to pray
They may be brought to see the light,
    And seek the better way.
And this I know, that great and small,
    And bad tho' they may be,
That I would save them, one and all,
    If it were left to me.

AWFUL SPIRIT.

GOD! who can Thee comprehend!
Without beginning, without end,
With no future, with no past!
Ever present, first and last;
In the great, as in the small,
Omnipresent "All in All!"
Nature's ramparts—hill and rock,
Men's great cities pass like smoke;
Time and nature shrink away,
But Thou knowest no decay:
All shall perish 'neath the sun—
Thou art the Eternal One!
In Thine everlasting now,
Awful Spirit!—what art Thou?

At Thy works, so great and vast,
Speculation stands aghast:
Everywhere infinite might,
Height still towering over height,
Far beyond mind's utmost sweep,
Deep still yawning under deep,
Heaven above, earth rolling under,
All is wonder piled on wonder!
Wisdom! glory! power unbounded!
Until reason stands confounded.
What of Thee can mortals say?
Silence is for things of clay!
Still we ask the "whence, and how?"
Awful Spirit!—what art Thou?

Artists ne'er can represent
Thy o'erhanging firmament,

Or the Morn, in robes of glory,
Walking on the mountains hoary ;
When the shadows hear Thy voice,
And the awful hills rejoice,
With their peaks in purple dyed,
In Thy smile all glorified.
Who can bring to soul or sight
Thy unfathomed gulfs of night ?
Or the awful shadowy power,
Looking through the midnight hour,
When repentance makes her vow—
Awful Spirit !—what art Thou ?

How can poet catch the tune
Rising from Thy groves at noon—
When each leaf and flow'ret sings
Of unutterable things ;
Who can note the full-heart strains
Swelling from Thy forest fanes,
Or the thunder, and the leap
Of the torrents down the steep ;
Or the laughter of the rills,
Or the silence of the hills,
Or divine the soul that broods
O'er Thine awful solitudes ?—
Or the calm on Ocean's brow ?—
Awful Spirit !—what art Thou ?

Turn we wheresoe'er we will,
Thou, O God ! art with us still :
We are never all alone,—
There's a presence in each stone ;
All the air is full of eyes
Looking on us with surprise ;
Sympathies run everywhere,
Thoughts are hurrying through the air,

Bringing near, related souls,
Though asunder as the poles;
Marvel upon marvel!—still
Miracle on miracle!—
More than proud man will avow,—
Awful Spirit!—what art Thou?

Yet Thine ancient bards have brought
Wonders from Thy realms of thought:
With their weird and wizard spells
They have wrought their miracles,
Started forms which make us start,
Things immortal as Thou art!
But those wondrous works divine,
Great Immaculate are Thine!
Awful things the prophets saw
In their ecstasies of awe,
In the body laid asleep,
Sailing the eternal deep;
Faith the helm, and hope the prow—
Awful Spirit!—what art Thou?

Dreamer vain and Pantheist,
May define Thee as they list;
As in childhood, we would rather
Look upon Thee as "Our Father."
High in Heaven, Thy holy city,
Looking down in love and pity,
On Thy sons of fiery clay
Fighting out life's tragedy.
We believe "Almighty Father,"
Thou shalt all Thy children gather,
Where the light eternal flows,
And no wand'rer asks, "*who knows?*"
Seeing not as we see now—
Awful Spirit!—what art Thou?

TO A VIOLET.

AH lovely little violet blue,
What language e'er can tell me true,
My strange relationship to you.

For, gazing on thy lovely face,
A living beauty and a grace,
A strange humanity I trace.

And yet thou mak'st me heave a sigh
For things that never meet the eye,
For things we'll know not till we die.

In the pure regions of thy smile,
We war above the mean and vile,
And everything that can defile.

Tho' springing from an earthly clod,
Thou tellest me of a bright abode,
Where all things lovely dwell with God.

Save for such visitants as thee,
How very weary we would be
Of this load of mortality.

Our spirits would be dark as night,
But for such gleams of beauty bright;
Thou living rapture, thou delight!

And thou hast come my lovely flower,
A visitant from Beauty's bower;
Her dew-drops on our hearts to shower.

And thou hast come to talk to me
Of that fair world where we shall be
From every sin and sorrow free.

And thy pure spiritual speech
Into my inmost soul does reach,
I feel—yet know not what you teach.

For, lovely flower, thou art arrayed
With feelings that can never fade,
And thoughts for which no words are made.

I vainly strive to fathom thee,
For thou canst only be to me
A beauty and a mystery.

STARS.

TELL me not of mighty wars!
Shut out the world and all its jars,
And leave me with God and the stars.

Ah, there ye keep your courses bright,
Old revellers in the hall of night,
Looking down on us with delight.

Ye, in that mystic vault were hung,
Ere mortals into being sprung;—
Before Greece was, or Homer sung.

At God's command ye rose in space,
Bright beauteous orbs, to gem, to grace
The portals of His dwelling place!

And priests, and prophets, sages hoar,
Looked up to worship and adore
In that old world which is no more.

Untouched by time, or tempest shocks,
Bright as when David fed his flocks
Among Judea's rugged rocks:

He gazed on you as I do now,
With wond'ring heart, and anxious brow—
Asked the unanswerable "*how!*"

We are the lords but of a day;
Ye saw Great Alexander sway
An empire that has passed away.

Where is he? echo answers "where?"
But still ye keep your courses there,
As bright, as beautiful, and fair!

Infinite temple! for no sect
Wert thou so wonderfully decked
By the Almighty Architect.

Yet all those worlds shall cease to be;
Yet, Father, thou hast given to me
The gift of immortality!

IF YOU WOULD BE MASTER.

THIS life is a struggle ! a battle at best,
A journey in which there's no haven of rest ;
And craggy and steep is the path you must tread,
If you would be master, and sit at the head.

The gods had their battles, they fought for their thrones,
They mounted up to them with struggles and groans :
And so the frail mortal must soar above dread,
If he would be master, and sit at the head.

O never strike sail to a cowardly fear !
And welcome for God's sake the taunt and the jeer.
And look at the devil without fear or dread,
If you would be master, and sit at the head.

Be humble and lowly, be upright and brave ;
Be often the servant, but never the slave ;
Submit to be bullied, but never be led,
If you would be master, and sit at the head.

The laws of creation insist on respect ;
Believe in the virtues of cause and effect ;
Trust only to truth, and you'll ne'er be misled,
If you would be master, and sit at the head.

Renounce all deception, all cunning, and lies,
Let truth be the pinion on which you would rise ;
Believe all deception is rotten and dead,
If you would be master, and sit at the head.

O SPREAD THE GLAD TIDINGS.

SPREAD the glad tidings! with rapturous voice,
Ye peoples and nations all shout and rejoice;
The long night of doubt and distraction is past,
And the bright sun of knowledge has risen at last.
We know that the soul shall immortally bloom,
For a glorious light has burst in on the tomb,
And death is no longer the angel of gloom.

The seventh seal's broken! the herald's gone forth!
Communion's established 'twixt heaven and earth,
With songs of rejoicing the glad tidings spread—
The dear ones are living we mourned for as dead:
They've changed but their garments, they've gone but before,
Tho' they left us to weep on Time's desolate shore,
Yet, they'll come to welcome us, parting no more!

To souls that are groping their way in the dark,
O, welcome's the dawn and the song of the lark,
And welcome's the beams of the bright morning star,
But this is a glory more welcome by far!
O dearer than sunshine! more precious than gold!
And greater than that by the prophets foretold,
Or all that was longed for by sages of old!

Then sing, for the dark veil at last is withdrawn;
Rejoice in the light of this glorious dawn;
We hoped against hope through the weariful past,
But faith's superseded by knowledge at last.
We stumble no longer 'twixt doubt and despair,
For we know there's a region surpassingly fair,
We know that the Summer-land's shining up there.

Then sing, for the wild reign of terror is o'er !
And the tales of earth's childhood can frighten no more.
Superstition and all her dark brood is o'ercast,
And the great King of Terrors discrowned is at last.
Let the voice of your gladness in anthems ascend,
Spread the tidings of joy to earth's uttermost end,
That Death is indeed poor humanity's friend.

Idyls of the Dominion.

INSCRIBED

TO

ALEXANDER MACNABB, ESQ.,

TORONTO.

Idyls of the Dominion.

"There is a pleasure in the pathless woods."
Byron.

ELORA.

LOVELY Elora! thy valley and stream,
Still dwell in my heart like a beautiful dream;
And everything peaceful and gentle I see,
Brings back to my bosom some image of thee.
I've roamed this Dominion allured by the beam
Of wild woodland beauty, by valley and stream:
From lone Manitoulin all down to the sea;
But found ne'er a spot, sweet Elora, like thee.

There's lone rocky grandeur away at the Sound,
And down the St. Lawrence wild beauties abound;
Quebec, towering proudly, looks down on the sea,
And lone Gananoque there's beauty in thee;
And Barrie! the lady that sits by the lake,
O, would I could sing a sweet song for her sake!
But here in thy beauty a-list'ning the fall,
O, lovely Elora! thou'rt queen of them all.

If friends should forsake me, or fortune depart,
Or love fly, and leave a great void in my heart;
O, then in my sorrow away I would flee,
And hide from misfortune, Elora, in thee.
Away from the world, with its falsehood and pride,
In yon lowly cot where the smooth waters glide,
I'd commune with Nature till death set me free,
And rest then for ever, Elora, in thee.

THE HALL OF SHADOWS.

THE sun is up, and through the woods,
   His golden rays are streaming;
The dismal swamp, and swale so damp,
   With faces bright are beaming.
And in the wind-fall, by the creek,
   We hear the partridge drumming;
And strange bright things, on airy wings,
   Are all around us humming.

The merry schoolboys, in the woods,
   The chipmonk are pursuing,
And as he starts, with happy hearts,
   They're after him hallooing.
The squirrel hears the urchins' cheers—
   They never catch him lagging—
And on the beech, beyond their reach,
   Hear how the fellow's bragging!

The red-bird pauses in his song—
   The face of man aye fearing—
And flashes like a flame along
   The border of the clearing.
The humming-bird, above the flower,
   Is like a halo bending;
Or like the gleams, we catch in dreams,
   Of heavenly things descending.

And hear the bugle of the bee
   Among the tufted clover!
This day, like thee, I'll wander free,
   My little wildwood rover!

Through groves of beech, and maple green,
    And pines of lofty stature;
By this lone creek, once more we'll seek
    The savage haunts of nature.

See there a noble troop of pines
    Have made a sudden sally,
And all, in straight unbroken lines,
    Are rushing up the valley ;
And round about the lonely spring ,
    They gather in a cluster,
Then off again, till on the plain,
    The great battalions muster.

And there the little evergreens
    Are clust'ring in the hollows,
And hazels green, with sumachs lean
    Among the weeping willows ;
Or sit in pride, the creek beside,
    Or through the valley ramble ;
Or up the height, in wild delight,
    Among the rocks they scramble.

And here a gorge, all reft and rent,
    With rocks in wild confusion,
As they were by the wood-gods sent,
    To guard them from intrusion.
And gulfs, all yawning wild and wide,
    As if by earthquakes shattered ;
And rocks that stand, a grizzly band !
    By time and tempest battered.

Some great pines blasted in their pride,
    Above the gorge are bending,
And rock-elms from the other side,
    Their mighty arms extending.

And midway down the dark descent,
  One fearful hemlock's clinging,
His headlong fall he would prevent,
  And grapnels out he's flinging.

One ash has ventured to the brink,
  And tremblingly looks over
That awful steep, where shadows sleep,
  And mists at noonday hover.
But further in the woods we go,
  Through beech and maple valleys,
And elms that stand like patriarchs grand,
  In long dark leafy alleys.

Away, away! from blue-eyed day,
  The sunshine and the meadows;
We find our way, at noon of day,
  Within the Hall of Shadows.
How like a great cathedral vast!
  With creeping vines roofed over,
While shadows dim, with faces grim,
  Far in the distance hover.

Among the old cathedral aisles,
  And Gothic arches bending.
And ever in the sacred pales,
  The twilight gloom descending.
And let me turn where'er I will,
  A step is aye pursuing;
And there's an eye upon me still,
  That's watching all I'm doing.

And in the centre, there's a pool,
  And by that pool is sitting.
A shape of Fear with shadows drear
  For ever round her flitting.

Why is her face so full of woe?
  So hopeless and dejected?
Sees she but there in her despair,
  Nought but herself reflected?

Is it the gloom within my heart,
  Or lingering superstition,
Which draws me here three times a year
  To this weird apparition?
I cannot tell what it may be,
  I only know that seeing
That shape of Fear, draws me more near
  The secret soul of being.

O! COME TO THE GREENWOOD SHADE.

O! COME to the greenwood shade,
   Away from the city's din,
From the heartless strife of trade,
   And the fumes of beer and gin;
Where commerce spreads her fleets,
   Where bloated luxury lies,
And Want as she prowls the streets,
   Looks on with her wolfish eyes.

From the city with its sin,
   And its many coloured code,
Its palaces raised to gin,
   And its temples reared to God;
Its cellars dark and dank,
   Where never a sunbeam falls,
Amid faces lean and lank,
   As the hungry-looking walls.

Its festering pits of woe,
   Its teeming earthly hells,
Whose surges ever flow,
   In sound of the Sabbath bells!
O God! I would rather be
   An Indian in the wood,
And range through the forest free,
   In search of my daily food.

O! rather would I pursue,
   The wolf and the grizzly bear,
Than toil for the thankless few,
   In those seething pits of care;

Here winter's breath is rude,
 And his fingers cold and wan ;
But what is his wildest mood,
 To the tyranny of man ?

To the trackless forest wild,
 To the loneliest abode ;
O ! the heart is reconciled,
 That has felt oppression's load !
The desert place is bright,
 The wilderness is fair,
If hope but shed her light,—
 If freedom be but there.

THE GIPSY BLOOD.

THE spring is here, with her voice of cheer,
    For the winter winds are gone;
And now with the birds, and the antler'd herds,
    My roving fit comes on.
I long to be in th' forest free
    From civilization's chains;
For there's surely a flood of the Gipsy blood
    Still running in my veins!

My soul is sick of this smoke and brick,
    I long for a breath that's free;
The desert air, and the hunter's fare,
    The woods, the woods for me!
Where things unbroke by curb, or yoke,
    Bound through the green domains;
For there's surely a flood of the Gipsy blood
    Still running in my veins!

I'm sick of trade, for its ways have made
    These artificial men;
I long to be with the wild and free,
    In the trackless savage glen.
For all my life has been a strife
    With their bridles, curbs, and chains;
For there's a flood of the Gipsy blood
    Still running in my veins!

O! why should I moil, and strain and toil
    For the lifeless things of art?

While the greenwood bowers, and the wildwood flowers
    Are springing in my heart—
Yes, deep in my heart, devoid of art
    A savage spot remains;
For there's a flood of the Gipsy blood
    Still running in my veins!

Let who may dwell, to buy and sell,
    I'm off with the roving clan;
For what are your gains, but curbs and chains
    To the freeborn soul of man?
I'm off and away with the joyous May,
    To freedom's glorious fanes;
For there's a flood of the Gipsy blood
    Still running in my veins!

THE SETTLER'S SABBATH DAY.

WELCOME to the weary worn !
Welcome to the heart forlorn !
Welcome, sacred Sabbath morn !

Peace from yonder clouds descending,
Heaven and earth again are blending,
And the woods in worship bending.

Yonder distant hill-pines lie
On the bosom of the sky,
Musing on things deep and high.

Yea, the very swamp has caught
Something like a holy thought,
And its face with love is fraught.

While yon ancient elms extend
Their great arms, and arch and blend
Into cloisters without end.

Forming many a still retreat,
Where the noon-tide shadows meet,
Ever on their noiseless feet.

Blessed Morn ! thou'rt welcome here
To the backwoods Pioneer,
Far from all his heart holds dear.

He has wandered far away
From the land of mountains grey,
Where his children are at play :

Urged by independence on,
Far into these wilds unknown,
He has ventured all alone.

Freedom whispered in his breast,
He would find a home of rest
In the forests of the west.

But he found it hard to part
From the partner of his heart,
In that cottage by the Cart.

And his little children three,
Crowding all around his knee,
Whom he never more might see.

In his log-built cabin rude,
In the forest solitude,
There he sits in thoughtful mood.

"Who," he asks, "at God's behest
Will lead forth His poor oppressed
To this Refuge in the West?

"While these wilds cry out for toil,
To produce their corn and oil,
Men starve on their native soil!

"Willing hearts are left to wither,
Bring, O, bring the workers hither!
Bring the lands and hands together."

From such thoughts he turns away,
For on this, God's Holy Day,
He would hear what prophets say.

Even Burns, he puts aside!
Burns! his week-day joy and pride,
Burns! so human, wild and wide.

And he brings from out its nook,
That great Book of books, the Book !
On its sacred page to look.

Now some song of Israel's King
Comes as on an angel's wing,
Through his very soul to sing :

Songs, that bring a joy untold !
Songs, more precious far than gold !
Songs, that never can grow old !

Sung by martyrs in the glen,
And in sorrow's darkest den
Cheer the souls of weary men.

Now he reads the tragic story,
How the world in sin grown hoary,
Crucified the Son of Glory :

He—the hope of every clime,
He—the sole bright star in time,
Solitary soul sublime !

Then his knee to Heaven he bends,
For his children and his friends,
All his soul in prayer ascends.

May God guide them o'er the deep,
As a shepherd guides his sheep,
Once more to his arms to leap !

Now he prays for all in pain,
For the wretched and insane,
And his tears they fall like rain :

Pleading for the sons of crime,
The despised, the dross, the slime,—
Wretched, Lord in every clime.

For the outcast in his lair,
All that need a brother's care,
Houseless vagrants everywhere!

Prays that mists may cease to blind
Fellow-workmen left behind,
" May they, Lord, have strength of mind

" To resist the drunken feast,
Scorning all that has increased
Their relation to the beast.

" Let their worth appear in deeds,
Not in whining of their needs,
Or in mouthing of the creeds.

" Let them try to fill the ditch
That divides the poor and rich,
Like a seething lake of pitch.

" Ever doing what they can,
Working out each noble plan,
Calling forth the God in Man!

" Break, O Lord! the spell of birth,
Haste the time when moral worth
Shall take highest rank on earth.

" Break the chains of creed and caste,
Heal the wounds of all the past,
Bring the reign of Love at last."

'Till the shadows lengthen grey,
'Mong the woods in dark array,
Thus, he keeps the Sabbath day.

A BACKWOODS' HERO.

[Canada is prolific in heroes of its own ; men who venture into the wilderness, perhaps, with little save an axe and a determined will, and hew their way to independence. Almost every locality can point to some hero of this kind, who overcame difficulties and dangers with a determination, which, in a wider sphere, would have commanded the admiration of the world. Energetic, inventive, sleepless souls, who fought with wild nature, cleared seed-fields in the forest, built mills, schools and churches where, but a few years before, naught was heard save the howl of the wolf and the whoop of the Indian. Who gathered, perhaps, a little community of hardy pioneers around them, and to which they were Carpenter, Blacksmith, and Architect, Miller, Doctor, Lawyer and Judge, all in one.

The following is a rough sketch, or portrait, of one such, with whom the author was long and intimately acquainted.]

WHERE yonder ancient willow weeps,
    The Father of the village sleeps ;
Tho' but of humble birth,
As rare a specimen was he,
Of Nature's true nobility,
As ever trod the earth.
The busy head and hands are still ;
Quenched the unconquerable will
Which fought and triumphed here ;
And tho' he's all unknown to fame,
Yet grateful hearts still bless his name,
And hold his mem'ry dear.

He hither came in days when this
Was all a howling wilderness.
With little save his axe,
And cut, and slashed, and hewed his way,
And scarce a moment night or day
His efforts did relax.

For at it, with a will, he went,
And all his energies he bent,
Determined to get through;
To him, all labour seemed but sport,
The Summer-day was far too short
For all he had to do!

He chopped, he logged, he cleared his lot,
And into many dismal spot
He let the light of day;
And through the long and dismal swamp,
So dark, so dreary, and so damp,
He made a turnpike way.
The church, the school-house, and the mill,
The store, the forge, the vat, the kiln,
Were triumphs of his hand;
And many a lovely spot of green,
Which peeps out there the woods between,
Came forth at his command.

What was it that he would not face?
He bridged the stream, he cut the race,
Led water to the mill;
And planned and plodded night and day,
'Till every obstacle gave way
To his unconquered will.
And he was always at our call,
Was Doctor, Lawyer, Judge and all;
And all throughout the Section,
O, there was nothing could be done—
No field from out the forest won,
Save under his direction!

He drew up deeds, he measured land,
For all the people thought and planned,
Did aught to help a neighbour;
He always had so much to do,

A BACKWOODS' HERO.

Folks wondered how he e'er got through,
With such a load of labour.
But something in his face said "work!"
The very dullest could not shirk,
The deafest had to mind him;
And if he only looked or spoke,
Or only said a word in joke,
He left his mark behind him.

All prospered where he had a hand;
The houses that *he* built would stand,
The seed *he* set would grow:
And for his bait the fishes fought,
The deer seemed willing to be caught—
'Twas strange, but it was so.
His plan of things was aye the best;
He carried success in his breast,
He had such art about him,
That, truly nothing could go on,
Wer't but the rolling of a stone,
It rolled not right without him.

Yet he would never follow rules;
Systems of colleges and schools,
To him were all unknown;
And in mechanics, and in trade,
His calculations all were made,
By systems of his own.
Few were his words, yet what he said,
Had aye the ring of "go-a-head,"
Improvement was his passion;
Tho' into order much he brought,
You always found him in a coat
An age behind the fashion.

A feeling heart was in his breast,
And cruelty to man or beast,

Found him a foe unsparing;
The two things which he could not bear,
That often made the good man swear,
Were gossip and tale-bearing.
New comers, when their crops did fail,
Would come and tell their mournful tale,
And he would fill a sack;
It always seemed to do him good,
To give a hungry mortal food,
And send him smiling back.

If roughs assembled at a bee,
And steaming with the "barley bree,"
They raged, and roared, and swaggered,
As soon as e'er his face they saw,
It held in reverential awe,
The most regardless blackguard !
He had his enemies, no doubt,
Such men, as he, are ne'er without
A brood of spiteful lies;
Tho' styled by some "The Autocrat,"
He paid as small regard to that,
As to the summer flies.

He sought not fame, nor did he e'er
Find fault with his too narrow sphere,
Tho' many a body said
" He was the man who should be sent
To rule our rabble Parliament,—
It wanted such a head."
And here he ruled, and here he reigned,
And no man lost by what he gained;
And here he lies at rest!
And may his mem'ry never fade,
And may the turf upon him laid,
Lie lightly on his breast!

SPARKING.

GIVE me the night when the moon shines bright,
    And the stars come forth to meet her,
When the very snow is all aglow,
    And the dismal swamp looks sweeter;
When the cows are fed, old folks in bed,
    And young lads go a larking,
And no one by with a prying eye,
    O, that's the time for sparking.

When all the "chores" are done out doors,
    And the hearth is swept up trimly,
And th' backlog bright, like a jovial wight,
    Is roaring up the chimney.
I listen oft, for his signal soft,
    'Till Tray sets up his barking;
For dogs as well as folks must tell
    When anybody's sparking.

I've sat with him till th' log burned dim,
    And the owls were all too-whooing:
For don't they spark, too, in the dark,
    Aint that their way of wooing?
I ne'er could bear love anywhere,
    Where folks were all remarking—
You act a part, but bless your heart,
    That's not what I call sparking.

At public halls, pic-nics, and balls,
    The lads will try to please you;
But it takes the bliss all from a kiss,
    If anybody sees you.
My old aunt says, in her young days,
    Folks never wooed the dark in;
It might be so, then Oh dear, oh!
    They little knew of sparking.

NEIGHBOUR JOHN.

THERE'S neighbour John, dull as a stone,
    An earthy man is he,
In Nature's face, no single trace
    Of beauty can he see.
He's wrought with her for sixty years;
    Believes he did his duty;
Yet all that time saw naught sublime,
    Nor drank one draught of beauty.

His only joy, as man and boy,
    Was but to plod and moil,
Until his very soul itself
    Has grown into the soil.
He sees no vision, hears no voice
    To make his spirit start;
The glory and the mystery
    Ne'er settl'd on his heart.

The great vault's hanging o'er his head,
    The earth is rolling under,
On which he's borne from night till morn,
    With not one look of wonder.
Talk not to him of yonder clouds
    In glory mass'd together,
John but beholds in all their folds
    Some index of the weather.

Talk not of old cathedral woods,
    Their Gothic arches throwing,
John only sees in all those trees,
    So many saw-logs growing.
For in the woods no spirit broods,
    The grove's no longer haunted;
The gods have gone to realms unknown,
    And earth is disenchanted.

In Day, with all its bright array,
    And black Night still returning,
He never saw one gleam of awe,
    Tho' all their lamps were burning!
Their seasons in their mystic round
    Their magic work are doing;
Spring comes and goes, the wild flower blows,
    And Winter's storms are brewing.

And Indian Summer steps between,
    In robes of purple gleaming,
Or in a maze of golden haze,
    The live-long day is dreaming.
John stands with dull insensate look,
    His very soul's grown hoary!
And sees in all, but sear leaves fall,
    And not one gleam of glory.

For beauty and sublimity,
    Are but a useless blunder;
And naught can start awe in his heart,
    No, nothing short of thunder!
He knows the world's a solid world,
    And that a spade's a spade,
And that for food and raiment, all
    The heavens and earth were made.

He laughs at all our ecstasies,
    And he keeps still repeating
" You say 'tis fair, but will it wear?
    Or is it good for eating?"
And we can only say to him
    "That it is very tragic,
To see but kites and appetites,
    Prowl in this Hall of Magic!"

FIRE IN THE WOODS, OR THE OLD SETTLER'S STORY.

WHEN first I settled in the woods,
    There were no neighbours nigh,
And scarce a living thing, save wolves,
    And Molly dear, and I,
We had our troubles, ne'er a doubt,
    In those wild woods alone;
But then, sir, I was bound to have
    A homestead of my own.

This was my field of battle, and
    The forest was my foe,
And here I fought with ne'er a thought,
    Save "lay the giants low."
I toiled in hope—got in a crop,
    And Molly watched the cattle;
To keep those "breachy" steers away
    She had a weary battle.

The devil's dears were those two steers,
    Ah! they were born fence-breakers,
And sneaked all day, and watched their prey,
    Like any salt-sea wreckers;
And gradually, as day by day,
    My crop grew golden yellow,
My heart and hope grew with that crop,
    I was a happy fellow.

That crop would set me on my feet,
    And I'd have done with care;
I built away, the live-long day,
    Such "castles in the air!"

I'd beaten poverty at last,
    And like a little boy,
When he has got his first new coat,
    I fairly leapt for joy.

I blush to think upon it yet,
    That I was such a fool,
But young folks must learn wisdom, sir,
    In Old Misfortune's school.
One fatal night, I thought the wind
    Gave some unwonted sighs,
Down through the swamp, I heard a tramp,
    Which took me by surprise.

Is this an earthquake drawing near?
    The forest moans and shivers;
And then I thought that I could hear
    The rushing of great rivers;
And while I looked, and listened there,
    A herd of deer swept by,
As from a close pursuing foe,
    They madly seem'd to fly.

But still those sounds, in long deep bounds,
    Like warning heralds came,
And then I saw, with fear and awe,
    The heavens were all aflame.
I knew the woods must be on fire—
    I trembled for my crop,
As I stood there in mute despair—
    It seem'd the death of hope.

On, on it came, a sea of flame,
    In long deep rolls of thunder,
And drawing near, it seem'd to tear
    The heavens and earth asunder;

How those waves snored, and raged, and roared,
    And reared in wild commotion!
On, on they came, like steeds of flame
    Upon a burning ocean.

How they did snort, in fiendish sport,
    As at the great elms dashing,
And how they tore 'mong hemlocks hoar,
    And through the pines went crashing.
While serpents wound the trunks around,
    Their eyes like demons gleaming,
And wrapped like thongs around the prongs,
    And to the crests went screaming.

Ah! how they swept, and madly leapt,
    From shrieking spire to spire,
'Mid hissing hail, and in their trail,
    A roaring lake of fire!
Anon some whirlwind all aflame,
    Growled in the ocean under,
Then up would reel a fiery wheel,
    And belch forth smoke and thunder.

And it was all that we could do
    To save ourselves by flight,
As from its track we madly flew,—
    Oh! 'twas an awful night!
When all was past, I stood aghast,
    My crop and shanty gone,
And blackened trunks 'mid smouldering chunks,
    Like spectres looking on.

A host of skeletons they seemed,
    Amid the twilight dim,
All standing there in their despair,
    With faces gaunt and grim;

FIRE IN THE WOODS.

And I stood like a spectre too,
    A ruined man was I,
And nothing left—what could I do
    But sit me down and cry?

A heavy heart indeed was mine,
    For I was ruined wholly,
And I gave way that awful day
    To moping melancholy;
I lost my all, in field and stall,
    And nevermore would thrive,
All save those steers—the devil's dears
    Had saved themselves alive.

Nor would I have a farm to day,
    Had it not been for Molly,
She cheered me up, and charmed away
    My moping melancholy;
She schemed and planned to keep the land,
    And cultivate it too,
And how I moiled, and strained, and toiled,
    And fought the battle through.

Yes, Molly played her part full well,
    She's plucky every inch, sir,
It seemed to me the "deil himsel,"
    Could not make Molly flinch, sir;
We wrought, and fought until our star
    Got into the ascendant;
At troubles past, we smile at last,
    And now we're independent!

THE MAN WHO ROSE FROM NOTHING.

AROUND the world the fame is blown
  Of fighting heroes, dead and gone;
But we've a hero of our own—
  The man who rose from nothing.

He's a magician great and grand;
The forests fled at his command;
And here he said, "let cities stand!"—
  The man who rose from nothing.

And in our legislative hall
He towering stands alone, like Saul,
"A head and shoulders over all,"—
  The man who rose from nothing.

His efforts he will ne'er relax,
Has faith in figures and in facts,
And always calls an axe an axe,—
  The man who rose from nothing.

The gentleman in word and deed;
And short and simple is his creed;
"Fear God and help the soul in need:"—
  The man who rose from nothing.

In other lands he's hardly known,
For he's a product of our own;
Could grace a shanty or a throne,—
  The man who rose from nothing.

Here's to the land of lakes and pines,
On which the sun of freedom shines,
Because we meet on all our lines
  The man who rose from nothing.

THE PINES.

I'M free at last, from the city vast,
    Away with the running brooks,
'Mong the savage woods, and th' roaring floods,
    And nature's glorious nooks!
The branches spread above my head,
    At my feet the woodbine twines;
All hail again! in your blue domain,
    Great brotherhood of pines!

Untouched by time, ye tower sublime,
    Aloft on your rocky steep,
Ye are seated there like lords of air,
    In your council chambers deep;
On your burnished breasts, and your gleaming crests,
    A quiet halo shines,
While the torrents sweep, and roar, and leap,—
    Great brotherhood of pines!

When morn awakes from out the lakes,
    Ye pour your holy hymn,
And when dying day in her mantle grey,
    With her phantoms round you swim!
No harp has the ring, and no sounding string
    Such a flood of song combines;
Old Minstrels ye of the greenwoods be,
    Great brotherhood of pines!

When storms are high in the midnight sky,
    And the wild waves lash the shore,
Afar up there, with your harps of air,
    Ye join in the wild uproar.

With the groaning woods, and the moaning floods,
   Your awful voice combines,
And the deep refrain of the thunder's strain,—
   Great brotherhood of pines!

By the torrent's brim, on the rainbow's rim—
   I climb to your magic hall;
To hear you join in the song divine,
   Of the thund'ring waterfall.
While through the screen of your golden green,
   A mystic spirit shines,
Hail one and all! in your magic hall,
   Great brotherhood of pines!

THE BACKWOODS PHILOSOPHER.

WELL, as I said, I'm forest bred,
    A rough unculter'd critter,
Yet, in some way, I've read per day
    A page of forest natur'.
Among the fust things I observ'd—
    My mates it didn't strike—
What ar we do, we'll nar get two
    That see a tree alike.

Folks may be honest and sincere,
    And may ha' eyes to see through,
And hold a principle as dear,
    Tho' they don't see as we do.
Now that's a very leetle fact,
    It seems as plain as prattle;
Would folks but see't 'twould save much heat
    And many, a many a battle.

Another thing which took my eye
    Was Natur's moral statur;
For Natur will not tell a lie,
    Nor won't have lies, will Natur;
A tree will fall the way she's cut,
    No words aside can win her,
And smash you splay, if in her way,
    Let you be saint or sinner.

And when you go to square her up,
    Nar heed what fools may say,
Cut to the chalk, aye, that's the talk!
    Let chips strike who they may.

He who would talk you off the straight,
    You tell him that he drivels;
The right is right! 'twill stand the light,
    Be't God's law or the devil's.

And he's no better than a fool,
    A little silly critter,
Who thinks by cunnin' to out-pull
    Or cheat Old Mother Natur.
Another thing which did me strike—
    While through the forest goin'—
Your timber's always somethin' like
    The soil on which it's growin'.

The elm will root em firm, I ween,
    'Mong rocks, and he will thrive
Upon the spot where maples green
    Could hardly keep alive.
And he will thrive and flourish thar,
    And to the winds he'll call,
And talk wi' spirits o' the air,
    Beside the waterfall.

Yon oak's exposed to wind and rain,
    To every storm that swells,
So every fibre, leaf and grain,
    His long life-battle tells.
He gathers strength from every shock,
    And tougher still he grows,
And looks defiance from the rock,
    To every storm that blows.

While far within the shelterin' vale,
    The lady-maple leans,
And tells her quiet peaceful tale,
    To gentle evergreens.

Close by, a brother all misplaced,
   In an unfriendly soil,
He fights and frets, until he gets
   Demoralized the while.

Then sad and lone, and woe-begone,
   To every wind he sighs,
Resigns the strife for light and life,
   And sullenly he dies.
So, like the tree, what we would be
   Depends not on our skill,
And wrong, or right, are we, despite
   Our wishes or our will.

OLD CANADA; OR, GEE BUCK GEE.

THE country's goin' fast to ruin!
This edication's our undoin',
We're comin' to a pretty pass,
Our boys who scarce have been to grass,
Have all gone off, bound to the teachers,
Or city clerks, or peddlin' preachers;
Our darters too, are quite Sultanas,
All strummin' on them cuss'd pianos,
And try to trip us up with rules
They've learn'd away at Grammar Schools,
And look upon the likes o' me—
Who nurs'd them criters on my knee—
As far beneath them,—Gee Buck Gee!

And then they're all Book Farmers too!
And they would teach me what to do;
Manurin', ploughin', drainin', seedin',
All farmin's to be done by readin'!
O Lord! O Lord! it makes me mad,
When every striplin' o' a lad,
And every edicated ass,
Who scarce knows growin' wheat from grass,
Must teach the like o' me to farm,
Wi' Latin names as long's my arm;
Them criters teach the like o' me?
Who farm'd ere they could reach my knee,
Aint it presumption?—Gee Buck Gee!

I tell ye what! them and their books,
Are getting to be perfect pukes;

And sure enough this edication
Will be the ruin o' the nation ;
We'll not ha' men, it's my opinion,
Fit to defend our New Dominion ;
Not one o' them can swing an axe,
But they will bore you with the facts :
I'd send the criters off to work,
But that, by any means they'll shirk :
Grandad to some o' them I be,
O, that's what riles and vexes me !
Ain't it a caution ?—Gee Buck Gee :

COMPANIONS IN SOLITUDE, OR REMINISCENCES OF THE BUSH.

THIS generation ne'er can know
    The toils we had to undergo,
While laying the great forests low.

For many a weary year I wrought,
With poverty and hardship fought,
And hardly had I time for thought.

In every stroke, in every blow,
In every towering pine laid low,
I felt a triumph o'er a foe.

Each knotty hemlock old and brown,
Each elm in thunder hurling down,
A jewel added to my crown.

If e'er my heart within me died,
Then up would start my stubborn pride,
And dash the coward thoughts aside!

And hope kept singing in mine ear,
" Be brave! for what hast thou to fear—
The heavens are watching o'er thee here:"

But fighting with those stubborn facts,
My spirit paid a heavy tax,—
My soul grew callous as my axe.

But still some wandering sympathy,
Some song—learned on my mother's knee—
Came with the bread of life to me.

Save, for those rain-drops from on high—
Those fountains opened in the sky—
My life streams would have all gone dry.

Until that time, I little knew
What books for lonely hearts can do,
Till spirits round my hearth they drew.

My cabin seemed a whole world wide !
Kings entered in without their pride,
And warriors laid their swords aside !

There came the Saxon, there the Celt,
And all had knelt where I had knelt,
For all had felt what I had felt !

I saw,—from clime and creed apart,—
Still heaving 'neath their robes of art—
The universal human heart.

And Homer, and Sir Walter Scott—
They entered in my humble cot,
And cheered with tales my lowly lot.

And Burns came singing songs divine,
His heart and soul in every line ;
A glorious company was mine !

I was a brother to the great !
Shakespeare himself on me did wait,
With leaves torn from the Book of Fate.

They asked me not of rank or creed,
And yet supplied my spirit's need ;
O, they were comforters indeed !

And showed me by their magic art
Those awful things at which we start—
That hover round the human heart ;

Fate, ever watching with her shears !
And mixing all our hopes with fears,
And drenching all our joys in tears.

They showed how contradictions throng ;
How by our weakness we are strong ;
And how we're righted by the wrong:—

Unveiled new regions to my sight,
And made the weary winter's night.
A perfect revel of delight !

YOUNG CANADA, OR JACK'S AS GOOD AS HIS MASTER.

I LOVE this land of forest grand !
    The land where labour's free ;
Let others roam away from home,
    Be this the land for me !
Where no one moils, and strains and toils,
    That snobs may thrive the faster ;
And all are free, as men should be,
    And Jack's as good's his master !

Where none are slaves, that lordly knaves
    May idle all the year ;
For rank and caste are of the past,—
    They'll never flourish here !
And Jew or Turk if he'll but work,
    Need never fear disaster ;
He reaps the crop he sowed in hope,
    For Jack's as good's his master.

Our aristocracy of toil
    Have made us what you see—
The nobles of the forge and soil,
    With ne'er a pedigree !
It makes one feel himself a man,
    His very blood leaps faster,
Where wit or worth's preferred to birth,
    And Jack's as good's his master !

Here's to the land of forests grand !
    The land where labour's free ;
Let others roam away from home,
    Be this the land for me !
For here 'tis plain, the heart and brain,
    The very soul grows vaster !
Where men are free, as they should be,
    And Jack's as good's his master !

THE OLD SETTLER'S ADDRESS TO HIS OLD LOG HOUSE.

MY Old Log-House, I love thee still!
    I left thee sore against my will;
My new house, finer tho' it be,
Can never be as dear to me;
For memory's spell is o'er thee cast,
And I must love thee to the last.
For life's first breath in thee I drew,
In thee from youth to manhood grew,
All early thoughts are twined with thee,
And thy o'erhanging maple tree!
It seemed to me no other place
Had ever half so sweet a face;
And on the winter nights and days,
No hearth had half so bright a blaze
Among the trees no taper shone
With half the welcome of thine own,
And when from thee I went away,
In sunny southern lands to stray,
'Mid all their bloom, my heart would flee,—
Mine own log cabin—back to thee!

Tho' now thy household gods are gone,
Still often I come here alone,
And, on thy hearthstone, cold at last,
I muse and ponder on the past!
Till parents, brothers, sisters dear,
In all their beauty re-appear,
Despite of death, the joyous train
Comes back to love me once again!
I see my father in his chair!
My mother with her knitting there!

The children crowding round, to hear
The stories that we loved so dear;

Or list'ning to that martial song
Which rushes yet my veins along,
Re-counting deeds of heroes bold,
In Britain's battles won of old.

And many a happy night I ween,
Beneath thine old roof tree I've seen;
For after every logging bee
The neighbours all would meet in thee;
For when the hard day's work was done,
The logging contests lost and won,
We gave ourselves to social mirth,
And banished sorrow from the hearth:
And ev'ry happy girl and boy
Danc'd till thy rafters shook with joy.
A thousand recollections rush,
And tears into mine eyelids gush,
When thinking of the manly race
Who first were settled in this place,
Uncursed with thought, which has destroyed
Our social joys, and left a void—
A dreary void within the heart
Which cannot be supplied with art!

And here, upon my wedding day,
No palace ever look'd so gay;
With evergreens and wild flowers dress'd,
You smil'd a welcome to each guest;
And well I mind the joyous cheer
Which welcom'd home my Mary dear;
And how the youngsters danc'd and sung
Until thy very rafters rung,
And all the world to me did seem
As floating in a blessed dream!

And here, while she remained on earth,
She was the sunlight of thy hearth;

And here—beneath thine old roof tree,
She nurs'd my children on her knee;
There, with the very smile she wore,
She comes up to me as of yore,
As if she still would cheer the mate
She left at last so desolate;
And all the children, as of yore,
Are romping round her on the floor;
There Mary! with her eyes of blue,
And heart so tender and so true,—
Who pass'd to brighter worlds away,
While yet her life was in its May:
And Charlie, with his face so fair,
His large blue eyes and shining hair,
And ringing laugh, which seemed to say,—
"O, life is all a summer's day!"
I hear him singing in the lane—
"Royal Charlie's come again!"
How strange! that he so light and gay,
Was called the very first away.

But, ah! the vision's past and gone!
And I am standing all alone
Upon thy hearth all desolate,
To sigh o'er the decrees of Fate.

Thy walls are mouldering to decay,
Like all things, thou shalt pass away.
And here, the grass shall flourish green,
And nought to tell of what has been.
But sacred thou shalt ever be—
No hand unfix thine old roof tree!
And here I'll often come and sit,
While evening shadows round me flit,
Till as of yore the joyous train
Are all around me once again.

THE MAPLE AND THE THISTLE, OR RODERICK OF THE HAMMER.

A STALWART Scot, a tower I wot,
   Of sinew, bone and muscle,
Came to our land of forests grand,
   To give our lads a tussle;
For, in the land of mountains grand,—
   The lovely land that bore him,
As champion he still bore the gree,
   And carried all before him.

So Donald's challenge, far and near,
   The telegraph did carry,
At length it reached the willing ear
   Of Roderick of Glengarry;
Who's of a race that's no disgrace
   Unto the land that bore them,
Fresh as the vine, straight as the pine,
   Or maple waving o'er them.

This Roderick *Ban* has all the man
   In every limb and feature,
Not strength alone, and nerve and bone,
   But Science, Art and Nature!
Tho' Donald is as steeve a chiel
   As stalks beneath the carry,
As an athlete, he can't compete
   With Roderick of Glengarry!

So Roderick dares him to the test,
   In any style he chooses,
The canny Scot can not be caught,
   And utterly refuses:
His reputation on a cast
   Wise Donald will not stake it—
For Roderick *Ban's* the better man,
   In any way he'll take it.

For Roderick's feat, it is a treat
    That's worth a long day's going,
Words cannot ring his mighty swing,—
    It's the sublime of throwing!
Transformed into a living wheel,—
    The demon of the centre,
He gathers power, yet guides the steel
    Where mortal dare not enter.

As if the whirlwind in its wrath
    Its awful power had lent him,
He gathers on his whirling path
    A terrible momentum;
While every heart is still as death,
    In fearful expectation,
He hurls it on its sounding path,
    'Mid shouts of admiration.

E'en while I sing yon mighty swing,—
    My Muse she reels and stammers,
As in a swound she's whirled around—
    O, he's the King of Hammers!
Ah, Donald, at your highest heats,
    You can't compete with Rory,
Nor throw around your greatest feats
    Yon wild poetic glory:

Which silences all empty vaunt,
    Deriving critic's clamour—
And henceforth he surnamed shall be
    "Fair Roderick of the Hammer!"
Long may he live to wear the prize*—
    The golden badge of honour:
Then join with me in three times three,
    "The Hero and the Donor!"

---

* Presented by the Hon. George Brown.

THE PIC-NIC.

NOW morning fair, with golden hair
    Is through the pine woods streaming;
And of a day of mirth and play,
    The youngsters all are dreaming;
No sound of axe salutes the ear;
    The ox set free from logging;
And neighbours all, both great and small,
    Are to the Pic-nic jogging.

The girls and boys how they rejoice,
    So merrily they're driving,
And far and wide from every side,
    In happy pairs arriving.
Bill's mounted on his idol there—
    With boughs he has arrayed her,
And boasts the virtues of "that mare,"
    To Dicky, the horse-trader.

Dick stumps him just to try a heat,
    "Come, bring your scarecrow hither,"
And in such loving converse sweet,
    They trot along together:
They pass along the ridge of beech,
    And by the hemlocks hoary,
And leave the noble troop of pines,
    All towering in their glory.

They reach the grove of maples green,
    Beside the winding river,—
Still at the song, it sung so long
    To Red Men gone for ever!
And it will leap and laugh along
    As gay and happy hearted,

And it will sing this very song
    When we too, have departed.

A table's spread beneath the trees—
    Some busily partaking,
While others swing, or romp and sing,
    All bent on merry-making:
The old folks talk about the crops;
    The little boys are larking,
And with the fair young creatures
    The lads are busy sparking.

They form a circle round the spring—
    The sparkling waters quaffing,
All poking fun, and ne'er a one
    Of all can keep from laughing
At am'rous John, still sparking on—
    At sixty-two a wanter—
Or roaring at the great exploits
    Of Bill the mighty hunter.

His treeing coons, 'neath Autumn moons,
    His fishings and his forays,
His great affairs with angry bears,
    His terrible wolf stories;
When Fred comes with his violin,
    By young and old invited,
With shouts of joy, the bashful boy
    They circle round, delighted.

Tho' he is but a backwoods lad—
    A native born musician,
What strains he brings from those mere strings;
    O! he's a real magician!
He plays a quick and merry tune,
    With joy each eye is glancing,
How he appeals to all their heels,
    And sets them all a dancing.

That mother with her joyous air,
　　Her baby how she dandles,
While Bill and Dick are dancing quick,
　　And shouting out like Vandals.
The chipmonk peeps from out the logs,
　　And wonders at the flurry,
And all amazed, with tail upraised,
　　Makes tracks in quite a hurry.

The grey owl opens up his eyes,
　　And looks in stupid wonder,
While, through the wood, the partridge brood
　　Are rolling off like thunder ;
The old coon's in the elm above,
　　Pretending that he's sleeping,
But with one eye, the old boy sly,
　　A wond'ring watch is keeping.

Fred's mood has changed, and in the midst
　　Of all our merry madness,
He makes us drink, ere we can think,
　　The deeper joy of sadness ;
The youths and maidens hush to hear—
　　Tho' 'tis no tale of glory—
And drink in with a greedy ear
　　That simple backwood's story.

His voice he flings among the strings
　　That seem with sorrow laden,
Oh ! hear the sighs, and wailing cries
　　Of the poor hapless maiden :
"Ah, thou art laid in thy death bed,
　　Beneath the grassy cover ;
Why did the tree not fall on me
　　Which fell on thee, my lover ?"

That wail of woe, so long and low,
    Is in the distance dying,
And there the rude sons of the wood,
    Are all around him sighing :
Yes, there they stand, the rude rough band,
    Untutor'd by the graces,
As spell-bound there by that wild air,
    Tears streaming down their faces ;

And while their hearts within them leap—
    Those hearts unused to weeping,—
O, what a silence still and deep,
    The maples all are keeping !
The grove is all a magic hall,
    And he, the necromancer,—
The master of the wizard spells
    To which our spirits answer.

Time steals along, with tale and song,
    Until the warning shadow
Is stretching seen, from maples green,
    And creeping o'er the meadow ;
Old folks begin to think 'tis time
    That they are homeward going,
And so they sing a parting rhyme,
    With hearts all overflowing.

The boys must see the girls to home,
    So they hitch up for starting,
And merrily they drive along,
    So have a kiss at parting :
As Dick trots home, that little song
    He can't keep from repeating,
While Bill declares, " them backwood airs
    Are good as going to meeting !"

TO A HUMMING BIRD.

HUSH thee, hush thee! not a word!
'Tis the lovely humming-bird
Like a spirit of the air
Coming from—we know not where!
Bursting on our raptured sight
Like a vision of delight—
Circled in a radiant ring,
O, thou glory on the wing!
Thou'rt no thing of mortal birth,
Far too beautiful for earth,
But a thing of happy dreams,
Rainbow glories, heavenly gleams,
Something fallen from out the sky,
To delight man's heart and eye,
In this weary world of ours—
Wand'ring spirit of the flowers!

Thou'rt a wonder and a joy
To that happy little boy,
As, in ecstasy he stands
Gazing with uplifted hands;
In a rapture of surprise,
He devours thee with his eyes;
Thou shalt haunt him many a day,
Even when his locks are gray,
Thou'lt be a remember'd joy—
Happy, happy little boy!

Yonder old man's face the while
Brightens with a welcome smile,
Toiling at his daily duty,
He is startled by thy beauty:

Out of all his toils and cares,
Thou has ta'en him unawares—
Ta'en him in a moment back,
O'er a long and weary track.
Once again, the mountains gray,
In that dear land far away,
And his father's humble cot,
Round him in a vision float—
And despite of age and pain,
He's a little boy again.

Welcome, Welcome! happy sprite,
Welcome! spirit of delight;
Deeper than the joy of wine,
Or the ancient songs divine;
For my spirit thou dost carry
Back into the realms of Fairy.
Round my heart thou com'st to weave
Things we hope for and believe,
Things we've longed for since our birth,
Things we've never found on earth;
O how weary would we be,
Save for visitants like thee!

But, like pleasure, lovely thing,
Thou art ever on the wing;
Like the things we wish to stay,
Thou'rt the first to pass away—
Flying like our hopes the fleetest,
Passing like the joy that's sweetest;
Even now like music's tone,
Thou'rt a glory come and gone.

"WEE DAVIE LOW."

[A boy eight years of age, residing at Edmonton, who accidentally lost both of his arms by a reaping machine.]

THIS world's a medley of joy and of woe,
Of wealth and of want, of the high and the low ;
Some dancing and tripping to mirth's joyous strain,
While others are writhing in anguish and pain ;
There are some never taste of misfortune's sad cup,
Others destined to drink, yea, its very dregs up !
A strange panorama still moving along,
With big hearts and small ones, with right and with wrong.
With saint and with sinner, with wise man and clown,
And those up to-day may to-morrow be down ;
What may be awaiting us, no one can know,—
The humble exalted, the proud be laid low ;
We're all God's poor children dependent alike,
There are none raised so high that His arm cannot strike.
And it ought to humble the high haughty brow,
To think of such sufferers as WEE DAVIE LOW.

His life has been blasted, poor boy ! at the start,
And nothing can help him in science or art ;
Unarmed, all unfit for the battle of life,
To him it must be a long terrible strife ;
The sweet joys of childhood he never can know,
Its games, and its gambols, he'll have to forego ;
And then, what a terrible prospect ahead !
Through life like a babe to be tended and fed,
Well might it be written upon his young brow—
"There have few been afflicted like WEE DAVIE LOW."

God gives his unfortunates into our care,
He gives us our strength, just their burdens to bear;
When fortune smiles on us, and joys overflow,
Let us never forget there are others in woe;
In the struggle for honour, for power or for pelf,
Let us still have a few thoughts that soar above self!
Of all human beings, they're surely the best,
Who cheer the forsaken, and shield the oppressed;
And Christ was not found 'mong the great and the famed;
He went 'mong the poor, the despised, and the maimed;
He was found with His great heart and meek humble brow,
Bringing comfort to sufferers like WEE DAVIE LOW!

When Death comes at last, as he'll come to us all!
And these garments of flesh from the spirit shall fall,
The question won't be then—" Of what sect were you?"
But, " For my afflicted ones what did ye do?"
Did ye soothe the forsaken when hope did depart?
Did ye drop the warm balm on the poor bleeding heart?
Did ye lighten the burden, and bathe the sad brow
Of poor little sufferers like WEE DAVIE LOW?

This world shall perish, and pass like a breath,
But our deeds they shall follow us even in death!
If bad, they shall dog us behind the dark veil,
And with their reproaches our spirits assail!
If good, they're eternal and never can fade,—
Of them the bright mansions immortal are made!
Words spoken in kindness, the tear and the sigh,
Are the gems that adorn the bright mansions on high,
And charity turns to a wreath on the brow,
When given to sufferers like WEE DAVIE LOW.

SPRING.

COME let us sing! for the merry Spring
    Is here with her joyous train;
And the little school-boy claps his hands with joy
    For the blue-bird's come again.
The flowers peep forth,—for the smiling earth
    Her winter's chain is breaking,—
And all things fair, in earth and air,
    To life and joy awaking.

The insects creep from their winter's sleep,
    The air has a mystic humming;
We hear the beat of unnumbered feet,
    To the joyous revel coming.
The dark brown thrush leaves the lowly bush,
    And mounts to the maple's branches;
With joy he sees the budding trees,
    And into song he launches.

The squirrel too, makes a great ado,
    For he hears the song so mellow,
And sing he would, if he only could,
    For he's a happy fellow:
How nimbly he gets up the tree,
    And leaps among the branches,
Where proudly he looks down on me,
    And chatters on his haunches.

With burning breast, and snowy crest,
    The woodpecker loves to follow,
And how he raps, and tap, tap, taps
    On every heart that's hollow.

The pewee and the chicadee,
   The phœbe, and the swallow,
Are in the air, on pinions rare,
   Or romping in the fallow.

And there the crow hops to and fro,
   All in his coat so sooty;
And hear yon jay! despite his bray—
   O, he's a perfect beauty!
He knows it too, as well as you,
   And trims up in all weathers,
Just see him stride with peacock pride
   Of his collar, cap, and feathers.

Ah, Robin dear! you're welcome here,
   Come, tell us where you've been, lad?
How time has past, since we saw you last,
   And what sights you have seen lad.
And O, ye bands from southern lands,
   Of roving little fellows,
That duly here, with spring appear,
   Of mirth and joy to tell us:

Ye're welcome here! my minstrels dear,—
   My little wildwood rangers,
That by your star are led afar,
   To sing your songs to strangers:
Ye're a jovial lot! what a happy thought
   Aye with the spring to travel,
With skies of blue, the whole year through,
   And a never ending revel!

Ye come to cheer our spirits here,
   For there's a charm about you:
And oh! to me, the woods would be
   A dreary waste without you.

GOING TO THE BUSH.

THIS settlement is getting old,
    And just a leettle crowdy;
I'll not loaf round this worn out ground,
    Like any idle rowdy.
There's few like me, can fell a tree,
    I'm bully at the axe;
I'm twenty-one, its time dad's son
    Was up and making tracks.

Dad says, that when he's dead and gone,
    I'll have this farm of his'n,
If I'll but stay, and work away,
    Since market stuffs have risen.
That's too onsartain, and besides
    I'll never wish him dead,—
Not fond of pelf—yet for myself
    I want to go a-head.

I'll chop a homestead o' my own,
    The first thing that I'll do,
And raise a shanty right away,
    With room enough for two.
I'll hunt me up some neighbour gal—
    For I wont live alone;
And there in joy, without alloy,
    Raise chickens o' my own.

Now, let me see—who will it be,
    To whom I'll give the call?
I'll surely find one to my mind,
    When I've the pick of all!

I'm a six-footer in my socks—
   Tho' tanned a leetle yeller;
Yet after all, what gals would call,
   A rather handsom' feller.

Well, there's that Buckley gal—but she's
   Too slow upon her feet;
She'd be no use, back in the bush,
   With nothing but conceit.
There's Laura Larkings—she won't do,
   For she's both cross and cranky;
I know she'd shirk all kinds of work,
   Like any down-east Yankee.

There's Mary Ann, smart gal I swan!
   And good too, I consider;
But, then you see, it cannot be,
   'Cause I won't have a widder.
And there is Sal, a tidy gal!
   A favorite o' my mother's;
But then I would be eaten up,
   With all her loafing brothers.

And there's the Reeve's young daughter too,
   That gal's got quite affected!
And O, what airs she always wears,
   Since her dad was elected.
And how she squalls, at what she calls
   " Her sacred songs so charming;"
But, O my stars! them heavenly airs
   Are really quite alarming.

There's Liz—but she won't do for me!
   For she's her mother's daughter,
Whose tongue has kept this settlement
   For years in boiling water.

A handsom' gal tho' she may be—
　And very few are smarter—
We went to school, but could'nt pull,
　For she's a regular Tarter.

There's Nancy Ann, the gal I swan !
　Jist laughing ripe, and mellor ;
A perfect brick ! she'll do right slick !
　Lord, I'm a lucky feller.
I mind, when old schoolmaster frowned,
　And shook the blue-beech o'er me,
She took my part, and bless her heart !
　She lied like sixty for me.

Yes, Nan shall be the gal for me !
　A clever-handed gal !
I'll get her too, with small ado,
　I'm certain sure I shall.
Then here's for Nan ! she's mine I swan !
　And we'll have no delaying,
Hitched right away ! that's what I say !
　And start the first o' sleighing.

OLD HOSS.

YOU educated folks, no doubt,
    At spinning yarns are bosses;
Well, for some trade, each man is made,
    I'm number one at hosses.
I'm known all o'er the township, sir,
    By hired hand and boss;
As I go by, the children cry,—
    "There goes the Great Old Hoss!"

I often wonder—and to know
    I'm really at a loss—
What kind o' soul a man can have,
    That does'nt love a hoss.
I love the critters every one,
    And that's the way, you see,
That every critter 'neath the sun,
    A liking has for me.

If ever I gets badly riled,
    If ever I gets cross—
'Tis when I see brutality
    Inflicted on a hoss.
They knows it too, as well as you;
    And every hoss I meet,
Lor bless your heart! they nods to me,
    As I goes down the street.

A hoss sir, has ideas sir!
    And if you truly love him,
And educate him as you ought,
    You'll make a christian of him.

A hoss sir, will be good or bad,
    It's all in how you break him;
He'll be a christian or a brute,
    Just as you've sense to make him.

For be we either man or hoss,
    We've all an inborn sin:
And what is Christianity?
    But just a breaking in.
Now, I gives all my hosses, sir,
    A christian education;
And nar a one but has some sense
    Of moral obligation.

You see, the first thing that I does,
    I lets them know I'm boss,
All in love too! that's how I do,—
    A woman or a hoss.
A hoss knows what a feller is,
    Whene'er he meets his eyes;
And there he'll take, and no mistake!
    His measure and his size.

He knows a man, that is a man,
    And feels that he's his master;
Detects a knave, or coward slave,
    No woman does it faster!
He hates them blust'ring bullies, sir,
    Them fellows that are gross;
Be good yourself, if you would be
    Respected by a hoss!

No doubt at times, as 'mong ourselves,
    You'll come across a fool,
He'll try your temper fearfully,
    But you must just keep cool.

I've had some heart-breaks in my time—
   Some awful stupid asses!
To make them moral animals,
   All human skill surpasses.

For you may treat them as you may,
   They're crooked as a fence;
In man or hoss, the want o' wants,
   Is want o' common sense!
But really in a common way,
   I'm very seldom beat;
And as I say, thanked every day,
   When walking down the street.

YOUNG HOSS.

NOW here's a hoss, that is a hoss!
    Most folks are of opinion,
There isn't such another hoss
    In all our great Dominion.
See, how he paces like a prince!
    He's willing, and no schemer;
And at a race, or trotting pace,
    I tell you, he's a screamer!

To see me driving past the mail,
    To reach the railway station,
And leaving it both head and tail,—
    I tell ye, it's a caution.
And them old farmers, with their wheat,
    They're to the market teaming;
How hopefully they jog along,
    Of mighty prices dreaming!

I like to see them old coons riled—
    They're always plaguey bosses!
You may insult them if you will—
    But do'nt insult their hosses.
I drives up quietly behind,
    And if there's aught like sleighing—
I gives the whip, and like a ship,
    I passes them hurrahing!

A mighty swell came out from town,
    And boasted, O, tarnation!—
His mare would trot the township down,
    And gallop all creation.

And how he swaggered all around;
    Stumped everyone about him;
Thinks I, the clown, I'll do him brown !
    I'll take the conceit out him.

We tabl'd down a x a-piece,
    And started off like thunder;
Past him I flew, with small ado,
    Which made the critter wonder.
And there the miller's daughter stood,
    And how she laughed, O—cricky !
As she would bust, to see me fust,
    And roared out, " well done Dickie !"

A gal so sensible as Sal,
    You'll seldom come across, sir ;—
For ignorant's the most o' gals;
    But well she knows a hoss, sir.
And a tarnation handsom' gal—
    A regular romping filly ;
And all the other gals in town,
    Beside her look so silly.

There's something in her, when she's rigg'd
    For " Sunday go to meeting ;"
I feels abash'd, for—O be-dashed—
    She sets my heart a-beatin'.
And she knows how to hold the reins—
    Tho' Dandy's against her striving ;
You have to see't, it's so complete,
    O Lord, to see her driving !

With saddle, or without it, she
    Can ride a hoss quite handy ;
I tell ye it's a sight to see
    Her mounted upon Dandy.

YOUNG HOSS.

We two would work in harness well,
　And that I often tell her;
And faith, I think, she likes it well,
　She loves a smart young feller.

Them fools of fellers up the town,
　They need not round her slaver—
For I've it fixed for April next,
　And I'm the boy will have her!

THE DEATH OF THE OX.

AND thou art gone, my poor dumb friend! thy troubles
  all are past;
A faithful friend thou wert indeed, e'en to the very last!
And thou wert the prop of my house, my children's pride
  and pet,—
Who now will help to free me from this weary load of debt?

Here, single-handed, in the bush I battled on for years,
My heart sometimes buoyed up with hope, sometimes bowed
  down with fears.
I had misfortunes not a few, e'en from the very first!
But take them altogether, "Bright," thy death's the very
  worst!

My great ambition's always been, to owe no man a cent;
To compass that, by honest toil, my every nerve I've bent;
Not for proud Independence! no, of which the poets sing,
But for the very love of Right—the justice of the thing.

To clear accounts within the year, I saw my way so plain—
But losing thee, it throws me back, God knows, how far
  again!
Just when I thought within my grasp, I had success secure,
Here comes Misfortune back again, resolved to keep me
  poor!

I've no one to depend upon, to do my teaming now!
And there's ten acres to be logged! the fallow all to plough!
How can I ever clear the land—how can I drag the wheat?
How can I keep my credit clear—how can my children eat?

O, nothing in the shape of work, was e'er a scare to thee !
Thou wert the hero of the field, at every logging bee !
The drags, they might be double length, the maples monster thick,
Then give thee but a "rolling hitch," and off they went so slick.

'Twas but a tug,—the monsters seem'd to thee as light's a pin ;
And how you wheeled them round about, and how you jerked them in ;
The very crookedest of all, would hardly make thee strain,
And from the teamsters, every one, fresh laurels thou didst gain.

A gentleness, a beauty, too, within thine eye did dwell !
It seemed to me as beautiful as eye of the gazelle !
And, how thy hide of tawny-white lost every shade of dun,
And its brown streaks to velvet changed, all in the summer's sun.

And through the Indian Summer too, transfigured thou didst seem,
A great dumb giant looking through her hazy amber beam !
And how you loved in Spring-time oft, to browse beside the creek—
When all the air was laden with the odour of the leek.

How you would stand and ruminate, like sage in thoughtful mood ;
Or listen to the children's shout, far in the leafy wood,—
While they were hunting flowery spots, where Spring had newly been,—
Or gathering lilies, red and white, beneath the maples green ;

Or, far beneath the tamarac's shade—where many a hemlock leans
Above the salt-licks, in the dell, fringed with the evergreens;—
Or climbing the o'erhanging bank, or swinging from the
 tree;
Or starting with their ringing shout, in search, old friend, of
 thee!

And laden with the spoils of Spring, they'd follow up thy
 track,
And wreath thy horns superb with flowers, and mount upon
 thy back;
And how you shook your tawny sides, in absolute delight;
And I have stood, and looked unseen, in rapture on the
 sight.

It seemed a miracle to me—for thou wert never broke—
How willingly you always came, and bowed beneath the
 yoke;
And when Buck—as he sometimes did—would take a stubborn fit,
Then, in some language of thine own, you coaxed him to
 submit.

It's clear to me, that thou hadst got some kind of moral
 sense,—
For never didst thou sneak, and steal, nor ever break a
 fence,—
And when Buck would leap over one, for he was ne'er
 reclaimed,
How hurriedly you stole away, as perfectly ashamed!

And thou wert so sagacious too, so sensible and shrewd,
And every word I said to thee, was fully understood.

No whip was e'er laid on thy back, nor blue-beech, never
 never!
While slaves and tyrants wrought and fought, we lived in
 peace together.

I've no doubt, but you learned some things, my poor old
 friend from me,
And many a silent lesson too, I also got from thee;
I ne'er could think thou wert a brute, but just a silent
 brother!
And sure am I, to fill thy place I'll never get another!

OCTOBER.

NOT in russet, sad and sober,
    Com'st thou here, beloved October,
  As in Europe Old;
Not with aspect wan and hoary,
But array'd in robes of glory,
    Purple, green, and gold.
Over continent and sea,
To hold the full year's jubilee,
    Thou again hast come,—
Borne on thine own fairy pinion,
To our dear beloved Dominion,
    Our green forest home !

O ye, who live in cities vast,
Aside your weary ledgers cast,
    Tho' 'twere but for an hour;
O come and see this magic sight—
This revel of all colours bright—
    This gold and purple shower !
O come and see the great arcades,
And catch the glory ere it fades,—
    Come through no sense of duty:
But see with open heart and eye,
This glory underneath the sky,—
    This miracle of beauty !

See how the great old forest vies
With all the glory of the skies,
    In streaks without a name ;
And leagues on leagues of scarlet spires,

And temples lit with crimson fires,
    And palaces of flame!
And domes on domes that gleam afar,
Through many a gold and crimson bar,
    With azure overhead;
While forts, with towers on towers arise,
As if they meant to scale the skies,
    With banner bloody red.

Here, orange groves that seem asleep,
There, stately avenues that sweep
    To where the land declines;
There starting up in proud array—
With helmets flashing to the day—
    Troop upon troop of pines.
Here, evergreens that have withdrawn,
And hang around the open lawn,
    With shadows creeping back;
While yonder girdl'd hemlocks run
Like fiery serpents to the sun,
    Upon their gleaming track.

And in the distance far apart,
As if to shame man's proudest art,
    Cathedral arches spread;
While yonder ancient elm has caught
A glory 'yond the reach of thought,
    Upon his hoary head.
But every object, far and wide—
The very air is glorified—
    A perfect dream of bliss!
Earth's greatest painters never could—
Nor poet in inspired mood—
    Imagine aught like this.

O! what are all ambition's gains?
What matters it who rules or reigns

While I have standing here!
Gleams of unutterable things,
The work of the great King of Kings!
God of the full crown'd year!
October! thou'rt a marvellous sight,
And with a rapture of delight,
We hail thy gorgeous pinion;
To elevate our hearts thou'rt here,
To bind us with a tie more dear,
To our beloved Dominion!

INDIAN SUMMER.

WELCOME! welcome! Indian Summer,
Welcome! thou the latest comer
   To the wood and chase;
Thee we hail with deeper gladness,
Even for the tinge of sadness,
   That is in thy face.
Young October's reign was splendid,
Old, and sear, her glory's ended,
   And to gild her fall,
Thou descend'st on nature hoary,
With a spiritual glory,
   That surpasseth all:
A glory that no other land
Has ever seen, howe'er so grand
   Its lakes or woods might be—
A glory even bards of old
Were not permitted to behold,
   In climes beyond the sea.

Down from the blue the sun has driven,
And stands between the earth and heaven,
   In robes of smould'ring flame.
A smoking cloud before him hung,
A mystic veil, for which no tongue
   Of earth can find a name;
And o'er him bends the vault of blue,
With shadowy faces looking through
   The azure deep profound;
The stillness of eternity,—
A glory and a mystery,
   Encompass him around.

The air is thick with golden haze,
The woods are in a dreamy maze,
    The earth enchanted seems;
Have we not left the realms of care,
And entered in the regions fair
    We see in blissful dreams?

O, what a sacred stillness broods
Above the awful solitudes!
    Peace hangs with dove-like mien;
She's on the earth, she's in the air,
O, she is brooding everywhere—
    Sole spirit of the scene!
And yonder youths and maidens seem,
As moving in a heavenly dream,
    Through regions rich and rare;
Have not their very garments caught
A tone of spiritual thought,
    A still, a sabbath air!
Yon cabins by the forest side,
Are all transform'd and glorified!
    O, surely grief and care,
And poverty with strife and din,
Nor anything like vulgar sin—
    Can never enter there!

The ox let loose to roam at will
Is lying by the water still;
    And on yon spot of green,
The very herd forget to graze,
And look in wonder and amaze,
    Upon the mystic scene.
And yonder Lake Ontario lies,
As if that wonder and surprise
    Had hushed her heaving breast—
And lays there with her awful eye
Fixed on the quiet of the sky,

INDIAN SUMMER.

  Like passion soothed to rest,
Yon very maple feels the hush—
That trance of wonder, that doth rush
  Through nature everywhere;
And meek and saint-like, there she stands
With upturned eye and folded hands,
  As if in silent prayer.

O Indian Summer, there's in thee
A stillness, a serenity—
  A spirit pure and holy,
Which makes October's gorgeous train,
Seem but a pageant light and vain,
  Untouched by melancholy!
But who can paint the deep serene—
The holy stillness of thy mien—
  The calm that's in thy face,
Which make us feel, despite of strife,
And all the turmoil of our life—
  Earth is a holy place.
Here, in the woods, we'll talk with thee,
Here, in thy forest sanctuary
  We'll learn thy simple lore;
And neither poverty nor pain,
The strife of tongues, the thirst for gain,
  Shall ever vex us more.

HURRAH FOR THE NEW DOMINION.

LET others raise the song, in praise
    Of lands renown'd in story;
The land for me, of the maple tree,
    And the pine, in all his glory!

Hurrah! for the grand old forest land,
    Where Freedom spreads her pinion;
Hurrah! with me, for the maple tree,
    Hurrah! for the New Dominion!

Be her's the light, and her's the might,
    Which Liberty engenders:
Sons of the free, come join with me—
    Hurrah! for her defenders.

And be their fame in loud acclaim—
    In grateful songs ascending;
The fame of those, who met her foes,
    And died, her soil defending.

Hurrah! for the grand old forest land
    Where freedom spreads her pinion;
Hurrah! with me, for the maple tree,
    Hurrah! for the New Dominion!

ACRES OF YOUR OWN.

HERE'S the road to independence,
    Who would bow and dance attendance!
Who with e'er a spark of pride,
While the bush is wild and wide,
Would be but a hanger-on,
Begging favours from a throne;
While beneath yon smiling sun,
Farms, by labour, can be won.
Up! be stirring, be alive,
Get upon a farm and thrive!
He's a king upon a throne,
Who has acres of his own!

Tho' the cabin's walls are bare,
What of that, if love is there?
What, although your back is bent,
There are none to hound for rent;
What, tho' you must chop and plough,
None dare ask, "What doest thou?"
What, tho' homespun be your coat,
Kings might envy you your lot.
Up! be stirring, be alive,
Get upon a farm and thrive!
He's a king upon a throne,
Who has acres of his own!

Honest labour thou would'st shirk—
Thou art far too good to work;
Such gentility's a fudge,
True men all must toil and drudge.

Nature's true Nobility
Scorns such mock gentility;
Fools but talk of blood and birth—
Ev'ry man must prove his worth.
Up! be stirring, be alive,
Get upon a farm and thrive!
He's a king upon a throne,
Who has acres of his own!

WHIP-POOR-WILL.

THERE is a lonely spirit,
   Which wanders through the wood,
And tells its mournful story,
   In every solitude.
It comes abroad at eventide,
   And hangs beside the rill,
And murmurs to the passer by—
   "Whip-poor-will."

O, 'tis a hapless spirit,
   In likeness of a bird!
A grief, that cannot utter
   Another woful word.
A soul that seeks for sympathy,
   A woe that won't be still;
A wandering sorrow murmuring—
   "Whip-poor-will!"

ONTARIO.

O, FAR away from my forest home,
In the land of the stranger I must roam;
And sigh amid flowers and trailing vines,
For mine own rude land of lakes and pines.
And I long—O, how I long to be
In mine own Dominion of the free—
     Ontario! Ontario!
In mine own Dominion of the free—
       Ontario!

The old school-house, is it standing still?
Do the pines still hang o'er the old saw-mill?
Is the maple tree still fresh and green,
That over our old log-house doth lean?
Ah! back to them all, I fain would be
In mine own Dominion of the free—
     Ontario! Ontario!
In mine own Dominion of the free—
       Ontario!

And does the blue-bird, in the Spring
Come to it, as of old, to sing?
And 'mong its branches build her nest,
And rear its young ones in its breast?
O, had I wings like her, I'd flee
To mine own Dominion of the free—
     Ontario! Ontario!
To mine own Dominion of the free—
       Ontario!

And what, tho' many do forget,
There's still one there that loves me yet!
I see her form, I see her face—
I hear her voice in every place!
And backward still, she beckons me
To mine own Dominion of the free—
     Ontario! Ontario!
To mine own Dominion of the free—
     Ontario!

And still, as a knock comes to the door,
Tho' disappointed ten times o'er,
She runs—but to find her hopes are vain,
Of her wand'ring Billy back again:
And back to her breast, I fain would flee,
And mine own Dominion of the free—
     Ontario! Ontario!
And mine own Dominion of the free—
     Ontario!

THE MAPLE TREE.

MAPLE tree, O, Maple tree,
O, thou'rt a pride and joy to me:
Of all trees of the forest green,
There's none compares with thee I ween;
And long may you stand so green and grand,
The joy and pride of our happy land—
      O, Maple tree!

And all the birds, they love thee best,
And sing the sweetest in thy breast;
And there's no shade, nor spreading tree,
The free-foot rovers love like thee:
And long may you stand, so green and grand,
The pride and joy of our happy land—
      O, Maple tree!

And in the merry month of Spring,
Ere yet the birds begin to sing,
O, how the school-boy shouts to see
The drops of nectar fall from thee!
And long may you stand, so green and grand,
The pride and joy of our happy land—
      O, Maple tree!

And maidens, on their bridal morn,
With boughs the festal halls adorn—
And children clap their hands to see—
And old men love the maple tree;
And long may you stand, so green and grand,
The pride and joy of our happy land—
      O, Maple tree!

And all our sons, where'er they roam,
Still twine thy name with thoughts of home;
Tho' far away from thee I ween,
Yet memory keeps thy branches green!
And long may you stand, so green and grand,
The pride and joy of our happy land—
      O, Maple tree!

AUTUMN LEAVES.

THE great woods of Autumn are solemn and sere,
 Like dead generations, the leaves disappear;
And the great winds are sighing, "Ye tarry not here."
Yea, like the leaves we are treading upon,
Here, we are now, and to-morrow we're blown
Into the vast and the vacant unknown—
      Gone! Gone!

Where we have come from, or whither we go—
Ah! not the wisest of mortals can know;
All is a mystery mingled with woe!
Are we but shadows of doubt and of fear,
Doomed for a moment to grope about here,
Then in the blackness for aye disappear?
      Oh, dear!

Do we but dream of a future sublime?
Are we but creatures of ashes and slime?
Creatures begotten, and swallowed by Time!
Never, ah, never! to merge in the morn,
Life, but a mockery devils might scorn!—
Better, far better, we ne'er had been born,
      Forlorn!

BOBOLINK.

MERRY mad-cap on the tree,
    Who so happy are as thee;
Is there aught so full of fun,
Half so happy 'neath the sun,
With thy merry whiskodink—
           Bobolink! Bobolink!

With thy mates, such merry meetings,
Such queer jokes and funny greetings;
O, such running and such chasing,
O, such banter and grimacing,
Thou'rt the wag of wags the pink—
           Bobolink! Bobolink!

How you tumble 'mong the hay,
Romping all the summer's day;
Now upon the wing all over,
In and out among the clover—
Far too happy e'er to think—
           Bobolink! Bobolink!

Now thou'rt on the apple tree,
Crying, "Listen unto me;"
Now, upon the mossy banks,
Where thou cuttest up such pranks—
One would swear thou wert in drink—
           Bobolink! Bobolink!

Nothing canst thou know of sorrow,
As to-day, shall be to-morrow;
Never dost thou dream of sadness—
All thy life a merry madness,
Never may thy spirits sink—
           Bobolink! Bobolink!

TO AN INDIAN SKULL.

AND art thou come to this at last,
 Great Sachem of the forest vast!
E'en thou who wert so tall in stature,
And modelled in the pride of Nature;
High as the deer, you bore your head;
Swift as the roebuck was thy tread;
Thine eye, bright as the orb of day—
In battle a consuming ray!
Tradition links thy name with fear,
And strong men hold their breath to hear
What mighty feats by thee were done—
The battles by thy strong arm won!
The glory of thy tribe wert thou—
But—where is all thy glory now?
Where are those orbs, and where that tongue,
On which commanding accents hung!
Canst thou do nought but grin and stare
Through hollow sockets—the worms' lair
And toothless gums, all gaping there!

Ah! where's that heart that did imbibe
The wild traditions of thy tribe?
Oft did the song of bards inspire,
And set thy very soul on fire,
'Till all thy wild and savage blood
Was rushing like a roaring flood;
And all the wrongs heaped on thy race,
Leapt up like demons in thy face;
And rushing down upon the plain,
You raised the war-whoop once again,
And stood among your heaps of slain!

TO AN INDIAN SKULL.

What, tho' to thee, there did belong
A savage sense of right and wrong!
In that—how like thou wert indeed,
To those who boast a better creed:
Repaid thy wrongs with blood and gall,
And triumphed in thy rival's fall,
Like any Christian of us all.

Like me, thou hadst thy hopes and fears;
Like me, thou hadst thy smiles and tears;
Felt Winter's cold, and Summer's heat;
Didst hunger, and had weary feet;
Wert warmed by kindness, chilled by hate;
Had enemies, like all the great!
Tho' thou wert no type of the dove,
Yet, thou hadst to have one to love!
O, thy Wenonah, she was fair,
And dark as midnight was her hair!
Thy wigwam was a sacred place,
And dear to thee, thy dusky race.
Ah, yes! thy savage imps were dear,
And they would climb thy knees, to hear,
And drink thy tales with greedy ear!

What, tho' a wild rude life was thine,
Thou still hadst gleams of the divine—
A sense of something undefined—
A Presence—an Almighty mind,
Which guides the planets, rocks the sea,
And through the desert guided thee.
The dark woods, all around thee spread;
The leafy curtain overhead;
The great old thunder-stricken pine,
And the cathedral elms divine;
The dismal swamp, the hemlock hoar;
Niagara's everlasting roar;

The viewless winds which rushed to wake
The spirit of Ontario's lake;
Did not its mighty anthems roll
Through all the caverns of thy soul,
And thrill thee with a sense sublime,
With gleams of that eternal clime
Which stretches over Death and Time!

And oft, like me, thou'dst ask to know,
"Whence came we, whither do we go?"
A marvel, ah, poor soul! to thee,
As it has ever been to me.
From the unknown, we issued out,
With mystery compassed round about;
Each with his burden on his back,
To follow in the destined track,
With weary feet, to toil and plod
Through nature, back to nature's God.
Mine was the cultivated plain,
And thine the leafy green domain;
Thine was a rude unvarnished shrine,
In form thy idols were not mine;
But ah, mine were as strange to thee,
As thine, my brother, were to me!
And yet they differed but in name,
And were, in truth, the very same.

Dreams of the hunting fields were thine—
What better are those dreams of mine?
Ah, my Red brother! were not we
By accident compelled to be
Christian or savage? We indeed
Alike inherited a creed.
We had no choice what we should be;
Race, country, creed, were forced on thee—
Red brother, as they were on me!

Then, why should I have loved thee less,
Or closed my heart to thy distress,
Red rover of the wilderness!

Soon must we go, as thou hast gone
Away, back to the great unknown,
Where, elevated above doubt,
We, too, will find the secret out.
Then mayest thou th' uneducated,
Be found the least contaminated—
From civilization's trammels free.
Who knows, poor soul, but thou mayest be
Exalted higher far than we.

GRANDMOTHER'S STORY TO HER GRANDCHILDREN; OR THE EVIL EYE.

'TIS forty years and upwards,
   Since first we settled here,
All in the trackless forest,
   With not a neighbour near;
And all through Jenny Thompson—
   For Jenny wished me ill,
For there be wishes, darlings,
   That have the power to kill!

For oh! if e'er that Satan
   Was in a thing of clay,
He was in Jenny Thompson,
   Upon my wedding-day.
When I stood up with Jamie,
   There stood the wicked elf,
Who tried to put between us,
   And get him for herself.

And with her eyes she cursed me—
   Her eyes that burned with spite!
I felt them darting through me,
   I could have cried with fright.
When I told Jamie of it,
   He only smiled at me—
For the ways of wicked women,
   He never yet could see.

I lived in terror of her,
   But Jamie he would say—
"Freets follow them that fear them"—
   And kissed my tears away.

GRANDMOTHER'S STORY.

But still, for all his banter,
  I lived in dread and fear;
And often I advised him
  To come and settle here.

I dreaded the wild ocean,
  I never liked to roam,
But then, along with Jamie,
  The desert were a home.
And we had peace and comfort—
  Tho' not unmixed with ill—
And but for Jenny Thompson,
  Might have been happy still.

'Twas in the depth of Winter—
  I'll ne'er forget the day,
The roads were badly drifted,
  The sky a sheet of gray!
When Jamie left that morning,
  There fell on me a fear;
The spirit knows, my darlings,
  When evil things are near!

And while that I was sitting,
  And knitting all alone,
As plainly as you hear me—
  I heard a heavy groan:
I looked up from my knitting—
  Lord, may we all have grace!—
And there stood Jenny Thompson,
  A laughing in my face.

And while I gazed upon her,
  They bore my love to me—
For in the woods he perished
  By the falling of a tree.

Oh! I was quite distracted—
  Could neither weep nor pray,
For there stood Jenny Thompson,
  And there my Jamie lay!

I bound his wounds so ghastly,
  And smoothed his yellow hair,
And watched all night beside him,
  And Jenny standing there :—
Arrayed as for a marriage,
  In bridal robes of green,
Her evil eye upon me—
  The body stretched between!

Through all that awful midnight,
  There lay the silent dead,
And there we two were watching,
  And not a word was said.
The terror has not left me—
  Mine eyes are nearly blind,
And there are times, I'm thinking,
  I'm hardly in my mind.

And ever since—my darlings,—
  That woful night and day,
I wish I were with Jamie,—
  I long to be away!
And all through Jenny Thompson—
  For Jenny wished us ill ;
And there be wishes—darlings—
  That have the power to kill!

MISCELLANEOUS SCOTTISH PIECES.

INSCRIBED

TO

GEORGE R. GOLDIE, ESQ.,

"MAPLES," CHATHAM.

Miscellaneous Scottish Pieces.

HALLOWE'EN.

RECITED BEFORE THE CALEDONIAN SOCIETY, MONTREAL, ON HALLOWE'EN.

EVERYBODY kens that spirits
　Walk abroad on Hallowe'en ;
And the little playful fairies
　Hold their revels on the green.
Everybody kens they're partial
　To auld Scotland's bonnie glens :
Not a lintie o' the valley
　Ilka green nook better kens.

Mony a shepherd at the gloamin'
　Scarcely can believe his e'en,
Coming unawares upon them,
　Dancing in their doublets green ;
Singin' sangs, and drinkin' dew-drops
　Out o' cowslip cups sae pale ;
Or a' riding on the moonbeams
　Doun the dingle and the dale.

Mony a chuffy-cheekit laddie
　　They hae wiled by birken shaw ;
Mony, a mony a bonnie bairnie,
　　On that nicht they've charmed awa',
Weel it's kent they watch o'er lovers,
　　A' their hearts to them are seen ;
A' their quarrels and their matches,
　　They mak' up on Hallowe'en.

Weel it's kent they're faithfu' ever
　　To the genius o' our laun,
And in a' her cares and troubles
　　Send her aye a helpin' haun ;
Them it is, should Donald waver,
　　Mid the battle's loudest din,
That keep yelling through the bagpipes,
　　Till he gars the foeman rin.

'Tis frae them the Scottish minstrels
　　Learn sae weel their melting art,
Get the magic words that open
　　A' the fountains o' the heart.
Nane can dance our Gillie Callum,
　　Sing our Scottish sangs, I ween,
Saving them wha've tippl't wi' them
　　On the dews o' Hallowe'en.

On that nicht, there's nae denyin' 't !
　　Mony a Scot, as weel's mysel',
Hae had moonlicht dealings wi' them,
　　Gin the truth they like to tell.
Weel, ae Hallowe'en at gloamin',
　　Drowsy sleep bow'd doun mine e'e ;
And, to my surprise, I wauken'd
　　Daundering on the midnicht lea.

HALLOWE'EN.

There the big horn'd mune was glowrin'
    Doun upon me frae the sky,
And the wee-bit stars a' tremblin'
    Like the tears in beauty's eye;
Suddenly I heard a rustle
    Down beside the lonely spring;
Gliff't was I, nae doubt, to see there
    'Elves and fairies in a ring.'

There they were, a sittin' singin',
    Blithely on the velvet green;
And the owercome o' the sang was
    'Hey for Scotland's Hallowe'en!'
Frae their lips ilk word was fa'in'
    Sweet as ony dew'y gem;—
*Kennedy himsel' ne'er warbl'd
    Scotia's ballads like to them.

In the midst a hoary matron,
    Wi' auld Scotland's spinning-wheel—
"Scotland's auld respected Mither"—
    Oh, I kent her face fu' weel!
Gazing on her rugged features,
    What unutterable things
Stirr'd my spirit, while above me
    Flapt innumerable wings.

Shades of ancient Scottish worthies,
    Heroes with the laurel crown'd,
Martyrs, patriots and prophets,
    Saints and sages, hover'd round;
All the preachers and the poets,
    All the spirits great indeed
Wha hae twin'd a wreath immortal
    Round our puir auld Mither's heid.

Kennedy, a celebrated singer of Scotch ballads.

A' the stalwart chiels wha perish'd—
    Perish'd! no, they never dee!
Scotland, 'neath thy bluidy banner,
    Wha lay doun their lives for thee.
Lovingly she gazed upon them,
    Proudly claim'd them for her sons;
And, with all a mother's fondness,
    Call'd them her "immortal ones."

Then she turn'd, as to her children,
    Exil'd far across the sea.
Saying, "Lads and bonnie lasses,
    That I nurs'd upon my knee,
Tho' the ocean rolls between us,
    Distance cannot hearts divide;
Still, in spirit, ye are with me,
    By the Forth, the Tweed, and Clyde.

"Tho' amid Canadian forests,
    Or on Ganges' banks ye be,
Or in Afric's wilds, ye ever
    Turn with longing hearts to me;
Tho' in distant lands ye triumph,
    Still for Scotia's hills ye pine—
Ever thinking of our ingles,
    And the Hallowe'ens langsyne.

"And the quiet of our Sabbaths,
    And our psalm-tunes' solemn tones,
And our altars, old and hoary,
    'Mid the grey memorial stones.
Weel I ken my early lessons
    Deep in a' your hearts are set;
Ah, the Bible and the ballads
    No, ye never can forget!

"Ne'er be Fenian fuks amang ye,
    Stick to country, kirk, and Queen;
And wherever ye may wander,
    Aye keep up auld Hallowe'en."
Even while she spoke, the grey cock
    Clapt aloud his wings and crew,
And or e'er I wist, the pageant
    Past awa' like morning dew.

CARTHA AGAIN.

OH, why did I leave thee! Oh, why did I part
  Frae thee, lovely Cartha, thou stream of my heart?
Oh, why did I leave thee, and wander awa'
Frae the hame o' my childhood, Gleniffer an' a'?
The thocht o' thee aye mak's my bosom o'erflow
Wi' a' langing that nane save the weary can know;
And a' Fortunes favours are empty and vain,
If I'm ne'er to return to thee, Cartha again.

When I hear the soft tone o' my ain Lowlan' tongue,
Ance mair I'm a laddie the gowans among;
I see thee still winding the green valley through,
And the Highland hills towering afar in the blue;
But the lintie, the laverock, the blackbird an' a',
Are a' singing—"Laddie ye've lang been awa'."
Nae wonder I sit doun an' mak' my sad mane—
"Am I ne'er to behold thee, sweet Cartha, again?"

When I hear the sweet lilt o' some auld Scottish sang,
O how my bluid leaps as it gallops alang!
The thumps o' my heart gar my bosom a' stoun,
My heid it grows dizzie, an' rins roun' an' roun',
My very heartstrings tug as if they would crack,
And burst a' the bonds that are keepin' me back;
But then comes the thocht—here I'm doom'd to remain,
And ne'er to return to thee, Cartha, again!

In a grave o' the forest, when life's journey's past,
Unknown and unhonoured, they'll lay me at last;
Aboon me nae blue-bell nor gowan shall wave,
Nor nae robin come to sing ower my grave.
But surely! ah surely! the love o' this heart
For thee, lovely Cartha, can never depart;
But free frae a' sorrow, a' sadness and pain,
My spirit shall haunt thee, dear Cartha, again.

SCOTLAND REVISITED; OR, THE WANDERER'S RETURN.

WHEN mony a year had come and gane,
   And I'd grown auld and hoary,
And mony a hope had proven vain,
   And mony a dream o' glory;
Then backward to my childhood's hame
   A weary langing sent me,
I found my native vale the same,
   But very few that knew me.

There were the hills my childhood saw,
   They look'd as if they kent me;
And well they might!—when far awa'
   Oh how they did pursue me!
And there amang the broomy braes
   I often paus'd and ponder'd
Upon the joys o' ither days,
   Then on again I wander'd.

At length our cot appear'd in view,
   O weel I kent the biggin,
There was the same o'erhanging yew,
   And thack upon the riggin';
And there the winnock in the en'
   Wi' woodbine trained sae trimly,
And up aboon the cosie den
   Reek swirlin' frae the chimly.

O how my heart leapt at the sicht,
   Till I could hardly bear it;
I felt as if I would gang gyte,
   For I was maist deleerit.

And hurrying to the sacred spot,
　　Ilk thump cam' quick and quicker,
I tried to pray, but in my throat
　　The words grew thick and thicker.

To hide my tears I vainly strove,
　　For nae ane cam' tae meet me,
Nae Mither wi' her look o' love,
　　Nae sister cam' tae greet me:
For gane were they, baith ane an' a',
　　The dear hearts that I cherish'd,
Gane, like the flowers o' spring awa',
　　Or like a vision perished.

This was the spot of all most dear,
　　Where all my dreams were centr'd:
And yet wi' trembling and wi' fear,
　　Beneath that roof I enter'd.
There was the place my father sat,
　　Beside my mother spinning,
An' a' the bairns, wi' merry chat,
　　In joy around her rinning.

There, in the cottage of my birth,
　　The same rooftree above me,
I stood a wanderer on the earth,
　　With nae ane left to love me.
Oh! I had often stood alone
　　On many a post of danger,
And never wept till standing on
　　My native hearth—a stranger.

I sought the auld kirkyard alane,
　　Where a' the lov'd are sleeping,
And only the memorial stane
　　Its watch aboon them keeping;

It only said, that they were dead—
  Once here, but now departed:
A' gane! a' gane! to their lang hame,
  The true, the gentle hearted.

O life, I cried, is all a woe,
  A journey lang and dreary;
Is there na hame to which we go,
  Nae heart-hame for the weary?
I cleared the weeds frae off the stane,
  And lang I sat and ponder'd
Upon the days for ever gane,
  Then weary on I wander'd.

PAISLEY ABBEY.

All hail, ye ruins hoary!
   Still stately in decay,
Rear'd were your aisles and sacred pales,
   By the mighty in their day.
We boast of our achievements,
   And smile at the ages mirk,
Nor seem to ken, they were mighty men
   Wha built this "Haly Kirk."

And here the mitred Abbots,
   In this their abbey gray,
For ages reigned, till th' glory waned,
   And the sceptre passed away;
But still their spirits linger,
   And love to hover round,
'Mid all the change, that seems so strange,
   On their consecrated ground.

And th' bell is tolled by spectres,
   At the hour o' midnight deep:
And deid-lichts seen the chinks between,
   Where the monks are all asleep.
And just as the moon is waning,
   And the woefu' east-wind raves,
The Abbots all, when they hear the call,
   Start up frae their lowly graves,

And stand round their ruined altar,
   In their robes of white array,
For the souls unblest, that canna rest,
   To kneel, to weep and pray;

And still, as she hears the summons
    Amid the Gothic gloom,
The good old Queen, with her regal mien*
    Comes forth her altar tomb:

To plead for the hapless friar
    Condemn'd through countless years
To weep and wail in the "Sounding Aisle,"
    And echo all he hears.
Then comes a kingly shadow,†
    The founder of this place,
And there he stands, with uplifted hands,
    And pleads for his hapless race.

And he looks to good St Mirin,‡
    But the saint can only say,
" They never shall reign in the land again,
    They have passed like smoke away."
Then slowly there arises
    A dim and shadowy train
Of souls that still, have a taint of ill,
    And the mark of an earthly stain.

And there are chiefs and barons,
    Each head of an ancient line,
With sword and dirk, as they did their work,
    In the bluidy days lang syne.
And there two wrathful spirits,§
    Like dark clouds hover near,
Montgomery stern, and proud Glencairn,
    Who kept the land in fear:

---

* Marjory Bruce, daughter of the hero of Bannockburn.
† Paisley Abbey was founded by Walter, High Steward of Scotland, the original progenitor of the royal Stuarts.
‡ The patron saint of Paisley.
§ The feuds of the Montgomeries and Cunninghams (See Semple's History of the Lairds of Glen).

With their Maxwells and Skelmorlies,
   Who did each other kill,
After a life of feud and strife,
   They look defiance still;
Or, they avoid each other,
   With a mutual hate and dread,
Or meet and pass, as in a glass,
   But not a word is said.

And there the great Lord Sempill,
   With the bard of old Beltrees:*
And ranter Rab, and piper Hab,
   Wi' the buckles at their knees.
And the twa auld droothie cronies,
   They canna yet forget
The sang and tale—to the beef and ale
   They look wi' a lang regret.

And there the youthful gallants,
   The lords and ladies gay,
That still must moan in their confines lone,
   Till their sins are wash'd away;
And there they stand, a rueful band,
   Yet they scarcely seem to know
How the licht o' love, sent frae God above,
   Should hae been their deadly foe.

And they wha destroy'd the Abbeys,
   And heap'd the priests wi' scorn;
Ah, they've had time to rue their crime,
   Where they ne'er see licht o' morn.
And there comes Jenny Geddes,
   And sits in her lang deid sark,
On her buffet stool, the pair auld fool:
   To sigh o'er that Sabbath's wark.

---

* Robert Semple of Beltrees, author of the celebrated song of Maggie Lauder and the elegy on Habbie Simpson, piper of Kilbarchan.

For a' wha grace resisted,
   A waefu' weird maun dree;
And they come to plead that the church may speed
   The hour that will set them free.
While a' the wee bairns unchristen'd
   Come up to the font to greet,
Till the cock does craw, when they, ane and a',
   Pass aff on their noiseless feet.

LORD LINDSAY'S RETURN.

WEEL I mind that happy morn!
When I blew the hunter's bugle-horn,
And the sound through the leafy lane was borne.

And the joyous brothers, fair and tall,
Came bounding forth from the castle hall,
With their ringing welcome, one and all.

And a sister came with her fairy feet,
The happy sprite of that green retreat,
Oh why! oh why! did we ever meet?

We rang'd the dells and the forest free,
And O, what a joyous band were we,
Happy as only young hearts can be!

No sorrow came to those bowers so green,
For we had no time to think, I ween,
On the what might be, or the what had been.

But I left them all for a distant land,
Where the lakes and woods were wild and grand,
But my heart still turn'd to that joyous band.

Aweary of fortune's fickle gleams,
I sat me down by the stranger's streams,
And waver'd away to the land of dreams.

Again we rang'd through the forest free,
And sang our songs 'neath the greenwood tree,
Happy as only young hearts can be!

When many a year had roll'd away,
And mine auburn locks were tinged with gray.
I homeward came on a joyous day.

And on to the hall I hurried fast,
And the green lanes knew me as I past,
And the old hills said "thou art come at last."

Again, as on the happy morn
I blew the hunter's bugle-horn,
And the sound through the leafy lane was borne.

With hope, and fear, my heart did bound
But no one came at the welcome sound,
And echo only answer'd round.

And I rush'd into the castle hall,
But I found for the true hearts, one and all,
But pictures hanging on the wall.

For the joyous ones were dead and gone,
And their names inscrib'd on a mould'ring stone,
In the village churchyard, old and lone.

And the forester was old and gray,
And he said, "that like the flowers of May,"
He saw them one by one decay.

And I sought once more the greenwood tree,
And I sat me down, and sighed "ah me!"
Sorry, as only old hearts can be!

SCOTLAND.

CALEDONIA! can it be
    A wonder that we love thee?
And tho' we be afar from thee,
    We place no land above thee.
For tho' in foreign lands we dwell,
    A sacred tie has bound us;
Our hearts can never lose the spell
    Thy mountains threw around us!

And tho' thy breath is cold and keen,
    And rugged are thy features;
Yet, O, my country! thou hast been
    The nurse of noble natures.
Who left us an inheritance—
    A world of song and story;
A wealth of sturdy common sense,
    And doughty deeds of glory.

But, Scotland! 'tis thy sense of worth
    And moral obligations,
Which makes thee mighty on the earth,
    A ruler 'mong the nations.
Does not thine humblest peasant know
    The truth of truths supernal—
That Rank is but a passing show,
    But Moral Worth's eternal?

Scotland! the humblest son of thine
    Is heir to living pages—
Heir to a literature divine,
    Bequeathed to all the ages:

Heir to a language void of art,
    And rich with human feeling;
Heir to the language of the heart,
    Its sweetest tones revealing:

Heir to those songs and ballads old,
    Brimful of love and pity,
Which fall like showers of living gold,
    In many a hamely ditty.
O, sing us sangs o' ither days!
    O' ruins auld and hoary;
O, sing o' langsyne's broomy braes,
    And Freedom's fields o' glory!

O, we may leave our mountains high,
    Our grand old hills of heather;
Yet song's the tie—the sacred tie—
    Which binds our hearts together.
Then here's to a' wha fecht the wrang,
    And may their hopes ne'er wither—
To Scotland, Freedom, Love and Sang!
    For they aye gang together.

THE SEMPILL LORDS.*

OH, let me sit, at the midnight hour,
    Where the Sempill lords are sleeping;
      While the moonbeams shower
      Through the ruined tower,
And the stars their watch are keeping.

While the wand'ring wind, like a weary thing,
Through the long rank grass is wailing;
      And the shadows lone,
      Of the warriors gone,
On the misty moonbeams sailing.

Ah, ruin sits in those lordly halls! †
Where mirth and joy abounded:
      Where warriors dwelt,
      And captives knelt,
And the harp to glory sounded.

Proud Elioston's a ruin gray! ‡
And none to tell her story,
      Save the winds of eve,
      That come to grieve
O'er the wreck of her ancient glory.

And where are the minstrels, old and gray,
Who sang to beauty's daughters?
      They have past away

---

* The estate of Castle Sempill, lies in the parish of Lochwinnoch, and, when seen from the heights around, is one of the most beautiful and picturesque scenes in Scotland. It was acquired by Colonel William M'Dowall, in 1727; he demolished Castleton, one of the ancient castles of the Sempills, and built a modern residence on the site.

† The Peil, once a fortress of great strength; it was built by Lord Sempill, in the year 1500, and is now a complete ruin.

‡ Elioston Castle, the most ancient residence of the Sempills, built in the year 1260, its massive walls, and arched fastnesses, are rapidly falling to decay.

Like the list'ners gay,
Or, like music on the waters.

And the jocund bard, of the old Belltrees,||
In his moss-grown grave is lying;
    And the songs he sung,
    That through Scotland rung,
On the echo faintly dying.

And lowly lies that warrior lord,§
Who oft so gaily bounded,
    On his dapple grey,
    In his war array,
While the trump to battle sounded.

There's no one left of that lordly race
That climbed the steep of glory;
    And their might's but a tale,
    Of a granddame frail,
And a ruin old and hoary.

|| Robert Sempill, of Belltrees, who wrote the well-known song of Maggie Lauder, the elegy on Habbie Simson, piper of Kilbarachan, and other poems.

§ Lord Sempill was along with Regent Moray, at the battle of Langside; for his valour, achievements and counsel, he obtained the name of the great Lord Sempill.

MARY WHITE.

D'YE mind o' the lang simmer days, Mary White,
When we gaed to the auld Patrick braes, Mary White?
    When I pu'd the wild gowans,
      And wi' a' delight,
    I hung them in strings roun'
      Thy neck, Mary White?

D'ye mind o' the sang ye wad raise, Mary White?
The sang o' sweet "Ballenden braes," Mary White?
    It couldna be love, but
      A nameless delight,
    Which thrill'd thro' my bosom,
      My dear Mary White.

O, that was a sweet happy time, Mary White!
I've ne'er had sic moments since syne, Mary White;
    When we look'd at ilk ither,
      And laughed wi' delight,
    And hardly kent what for,
      My dear Mary White.

We were young, we were happy, indeed, Mary White,
Noo care's strewn grey hair on my head, Mary White.
    My hopes hae a' wither'd,
      Wi' sorrowfu' blight;
    But still ye are green in my
      Heart, Mary White.

And, oh! do ye e'er think on me, Mary White?
Oh! then does the tear blin' your e'e, Mary White?
    Or hae ye lang wak'd frae
      That spell o' delight,
    And left me still dreaming,
      My dear Mary White?

'Tis often I think upon thee, Mary White;
For still thou art dear unto me, Mary White.
    For a' that this heart has
      E'er kent o' delight,
    Was nocht to the moments
      Wi' thee, Mary White.

Do ye 'mang the living still bide, Mary White?
Or hae ye cross'd ower the dark tide, Mary White?
    Oh, how this auld heart wad
      Yet loup wi' delight,
    Could I again see you,
      My dear Mary White.

I WINNA GAE HAME.

I WINNA gae back to my youthfu' haunts,
 For they are nae langer fair—
The spoiler has been in the glades so green,
 And sad are the changes there:
The plou' has been to the very brink,
 O' the lovely Locher fa',
And beauty has fled wi' the auld yew trees,
 And the bonnie wee birds awa.

Young Spring aye cam' the earliest there,
 Alang wi' her dear cuckoo,
And the weary Autumn lingered lang
 Wi' her lonely cusha-doo;
And peace aye nestled in ilka nook,
 O' the bonnie gowany glen,
For it's always Sabbath among the flowers,
 Awa' frae the haunts o' men.

How aft hae I paused in thae green retreats,
 O' the hare and the foggy-bee,
While the lintie lilted to his love—
 As blithe as a bird could be;
And the yorlin sang on the whinny knowe,
 In the cheery morn o' spring,
And the laverock drapt frae the cloud at e'en,
 To fauld up her weary wing.

And the mavis sang in the thorny brake,
 And the blackbird on the tree,
And the lintwhite told his tale of love,
 Far down in the gowany lee;

And the moss, and the cress, and the crawflow'r crept,
    Sae close to the crystal spring,
And the water cam wi' a laughin' loup,
    And awa' like a living thing.

And it sang its way through the green retreats,
    In a voice so sweet and clear,
That the rowan listened on the rock,
    And the hazel leaned to hear;
And the water lilies raised their heads,
    And the bells in clusters blue,
And the primrose came wi' its modest face,
    A' wat wi' the balmy dew.

And the hoary hawthorn hung its head—
    As lapt in a blissfu' dream,
While the honeysuckle strained to catch
    The murmurs o' that stream;
And the buttercup and the cowslip pale,
    To the green green margin drew,
And the gowan cam' and brought wi' her
    The bonnie wee violet blue.

And the red red rose and the eglantine,
    And the stately foxglove came,
And mony an' mony a sweet wee flower,
    That has died without a name;
While the burnie brattled down the brae,
    In her ain blithe merry din,
And lept the rocks in a cloud o' spray,
    And roared in the boiling linn.

And churned hersel' into silver white.
    Into bubbles green and gay,
And rumbled round in her wild delight,
    'Neath the rainbow's lovely ray;

And swirled, and sank, and rose to the brim,
    Like the snawdrift on the lee,
And then in bells o' the rainbow's rim,
    She sang awa' to the sea.

But the trees are felled and the birds are gane,
    And the banks are lone and bare,
And wearily now she drags her lane
    With the heavy sough o' care;
And fond lovers there shall meet nae mair,
    In the lang lang simmer's e'en,
To pledge their vows 'neath the spreading boughs,
    Of the birk and the beech sae green.

In a' my wanderings far or near,
    Through thae woods sae wild and lane,
There was still ae spot to memory dear,
    That I hoped to see again;
But I'll no gae back, I'll no gae back,
    For my heart is sick and sair,
And I couldna' bide to see the wreck
    O' a place sae sweet and fair.

THE WEE LADDIE'S SUMMER DAY.

AT the call of the blithe cuckoo
   In the leafy lanes o' June,
Wee barefooted laddies I trow
   We scampert awa' frae the toun,
To speel up the Hie-Craig rock,
   The haunt o' the hinny bee;
Like a troop o' wee fairy folk,
   Wi' our happy hearts gaed we.

And never was king upon his throne,
   So free frae every care,
For the licht o' our hearts on nature shone,
   Making sunshine everywhere.
We ranged the dells and the forest free—
   To our joy the valleys rang—
Or sat us down on the gowany lee,
   To drink in the wild birds' sang.

We kent the place whaur the blue-whaups bide,
   An' the howff o' the hoodie craw;
And the holes where the wee moss-cheepers hide,
   We kent them ane an' a'.
And O, a mair joyous band than we
   Was never aneath the sun!
While we howket for the hinnie bee,
   In his byke aneath the grun.

O then, what a feast o' the hinny blabs!
   As wee laddies only ken;
Sic nectar never cross'd the gabs
   O' the very greatest men.

We cared na' for sic sma' affairs,
    As their kingdoms and their crouns;
Or the busy world wi' a' its cares,
    An' its weary ups an' douns.

We kent that our joy wad never fade,
    That the world was made for play,
An' 'twas nonsense a' what the auld folks said,
    Of the sorrows on our way.
Sae we rumple-tumpl'd doun the brae
    Wi' our hearts sae fu' o' glee,
Or swung the lee-lang simmer's day,
    On the auld witch hazel tree.

Or followed the burn wi' its twists an' crooks,
    As it jink'd roun the spunky knowe,
Or sat us doun in the fairy nooks,
    Whaur a' the wee violets grou.
And O, what a joy was the wild rose tree—
    Awa' in thae lonely glens,—
And the glint o' the gowan's e'e,
    Which the laddie only kens.

Our hearts had the glow o' the violet rare,
    And the freshness o' the dew!
And the lilt o' the sang that filled the air,
    Frae the speck in the bonnie blue.
And nothing cam' our joy to mar,
    'Till the sun sank in the west,
And the laverock drapt frae the e'ening star,
    And the cusha socht her nest.

And gloamin' doun upon bank and scaur,
    In her mantle grey wad lie,—
And the great old Highland hills afar,
    Were leaning against the sky.

And the Craik cam' out frae amang the braes
  Awa' by the Peeseweep Inn;
And hame we gaed 'neath the gleaming rays,
  O' the red red rising mune.

Ah, happy hearts! we can meet nae mair,
  There's been changes sad since then;
If in life ye be, ye're changed like me,
  Into auld world weary men.
But the hived up memory o' thae days,
  Your hearts they can never tine,
And aft wi' me 'mang the braes ye'll be,
  And the happy days langsyne.

THE DEATH OF EVAN DHU.

THEY place the Chieftain in his chair,
    Beneath the aged yew;
And is this all that now remains
    Of the mighty Evan Dhu?

The plaided clansmen gather round,
    And gaze upon his face,
They fear that Death will soon lay low
    The hero of their race.

Vainly they tend and talk to him,
    In friendship's soothing tone;
The old man sits with drooping head,
    Unconscious as a stone.

"Go, bring the minstrel of our tribe,
    To sing the mountain strain—
The strain he loved, t'will bring him back
    To consciousness again."

And leaning on his staff, at length
    The aged bard appears,
And gazing on him, thus he sings—
    But scarce can sing for tears:

"A cloud hangs o'er Lochabar's wilds,
    Her vales are filled with woe,
The shaft has started from the string,
    To lay her hero low.

"Behold the mountain warrior,
   The chief of sounding fame,
Whose claymore in the battle flashed
   Like a consuming flame!

"But where, ah, where's the princely air,
   And the step so firm and true—
The eagle eye, and the lordly brow
   Of the mighty Evan Dhu!

"Are these the very hands which laid
   The Sassenach Giant low,
Who dared invade Lochabar's wilds,
   Full fifty years ago?"

But he heeds him not, he hears him not,
   And the weeping clansmen seem
Like fleeting shadows hov'ring round,
   Or phantoms in a dream.

Anon he sings the mournful song,
   Some exiled heart of yore
Sang, when he thought that he would see
   Lochabar's hills no more.

But he heeds him not, he hears him not,
   And the weeping clansmen seem
Like fleeting shadows hov'ring round,
   Or phantoms in a dream.

Anon he wakes—the battle cry—
   The Cameron's gathering strain,
And the light of battle flashes in
   The old man's eye again.

He clutches by his side, as if
　　To draw his ancient brand,
And starting from his couch, aloft
　　He waves his withered hand.

And shouts, "Advance, Sons of Lochiel!"
　　With all the fire of yore,
And seems, as waving in his hand,
　　The terrible claymore!

Great Chieftain of the Mountain race!
　　It was thy last adieu:
And Clansmen clasp the lifeless form,
　　Of the mighty Evan Dhu.

LOVE.

WE'VE muckle to vex us puir sons of a day,
    As we journey alang on life's wearisome way;
But what are the troubles with which we're oppressed,
If love makes our bosoms the hame o' her rest.

When love lichts the hearthstane, there's joy in the ha',
And a streak o' sunshine on ilk bosom doth fa';
The ingle blinks blither, affections increase,
And the cottage she turns to a palace o' peace.

Where'er she approaches, a' hearts grow sincere,
She hallows a' places, makes every spot dear;
For wrang canna breathe in the sphere o' her grace,
And hate flees awa' frae the licht o' her face.

Where'er she approaches, where'er she appears,
She comes aye to comfort, and wipe awa' tears,
To help on the weary, and lichten their load,
And cheer them wi' sangs on their wearisome road.

And O, her sweet smile makes the fallen look up,
It's the ae blessed drap in their sorrowfu' cup!
Then O may this heart o' mine never grow sere;
O, let me, 'boon a' things, hold somebody dear!

O, leave me but love—tho' my rooftree should fa',
And the gear we hae gather'd take wings an' 'wa';
For riches and grandeur, the things we hold dear,
Are a' but vain glories, that die wi' us here;
But love burns the brighter wi' our parting breath,
And lichts us, at last, through the valley of death.

THE LANG HEIDED LADDIE.

HE'S a lang heided laddie that Sannock o' mine,
 And sometime or ither that laddie maun shine;
It needs nae auld spae-wife his fortune to ken,
He'll be seen and heard-tell o' amang muckle men.
But bairns are no' noticed by big folks ye see,
That belang to a puir widow-woman like me—
But he'll gar them notice ere many years go,
And listen to him, be they willing or no;
And to his decision, he'll make them a' boo—
He's a lang heided laddie, our Sannock, I trou!

Alane, by the burnsides, he ranges for hours,
And he kens a' about the wee birds and the flowers.
He's off, ere the cock craws, awa' to the braes,
And he stays out amang them for hale simmer days,
To talk wi' the peeseweep and lane cushy-doo—
He's a wonderfu' laddie, our Sannock, I trou!

There's no' an auld castle that towers on the steep,
Nor a field whaur our auld fechtin' forefathers sleep,
Nor a bonnie wee burnie that wimples alang,
In the licht o' its gladness, immortal in sang.
There's no' an auld kirk, where the gray howlets cry
To the dead congregations around them that lie;
There's no' an auld abbey that sits in the rain,
In widowed weeds, sighing o'er glory that's gane,
But he kens mair about them than antiquars do—
He's a lang heided laddie, our Sannock, I trou!

Auld Birsie, the bodie that lives by his craft,
Ance hinted to me, that my laddie was daft;
I bang'd up and tauld him, that "him nor his weans
Wadna likely gang daft by the wecht o' their brains,
Or their honesty either." I gied him my min',

And the body can hardly look at me since syne;
The spite o' the creature was easy seen through—
He's a lang heided laddie, our Sannock, I trou!

It's lang been my notion, and proud wad I be,
My wee friendless laddie, a preacher to see,
I'd shear for the siller, I'd do any work,
To see my wee laddie, a licht in the kirk!
But he lauchs in my face when he sees me sae fain,
And he says, that he'll preach in a way o' his ain.
There are preachers, he says, "ne'er ordain'd by the kirk,
That do a far greater, a far better work."
I whiles think his doctrines are really no' soun',
But he lays them so like our auld minister doun;
It's a perfect delight just to hear him gang through—
He's a lang heided laddie, our Sannock, I trou!

He'll talk o' ane Plato, a great man nae doubt,
And heathens, that folks here ken naething about;
When but a wee totem, he'd sit by himsel',
And spier at me questions 'bout heaven and hell.
And to him, it was a great puzzle, he said,
To ken hoo this yearth out o' naething was made —
How three could be ane, and how ane could be three,
Was a thing, he insisted, that never could be.
Or why we should suffer for auld Adam's fa',
Or, why that God e'er made a deevil ava';
I was fairly dumfoundered, and puzzled to learn
How sic thochts could get into the heid o' a bairn.
But I hae nae a doubt, they cam' into his heid
Like the mumps, or the measles, or grew like a weed
That's soon rooted out by the gardner o' grace,
And flowers a' the fairer, spring up in their place.
I cherish the hope that I'll yet live to see
Him waggin' his pow in a pulpit sae hie;
Nae doubt he's appointed some great work to do—
He's a lang heided laddie, our Sannock, I trou!

HUGH MACDONALD.*

I LOVE to look upon thy face,
    And doat on every feature;
Thou humble, unassuming soul!
    Thou simple child of nature!
Thou lover of all lovely things,
    With thee 'tis always May;
For love has kept thy spirit young,
    Although thy locks are grey.

Thou wert not made for cities vast,
    Nor for the strife of gain;
And it was joy to steal away
    To nature's green domain;
To hie thee to the harebell haunts,
    And to the glades of green,
Where wild wood roses hang their heads,
    And hoary hawthorns lean.

To hear the cuckoo's joyous shout
    Come welcome o'er the lee;
And 'mong the purple heather blooms
    The bugle o' the bee.
To hide thee in the hazel howes
    Of some lone cushat glen;
Or scale the Alpine summits hoar,
    Of some old Highland Ben.

We love you for the love you bore
    The flow'rets of the wild;
You loved them with the artless love—
    The rapture of a child!

---

* Author of "Rambles Round Glasgow," "Days at the Coast," &c., &c.

You loved them as the lover loves,
    And from no sense of duty;
You loved them as the poet loves,
    And only for their beauty!

Thy "flowering fern" shall never die,
    Thy gowan's aye in bloom,
The lark is always in thy sky,
    The linnet in thy broom;
For poesy hath touched thy heart
    As with a living coal;
And nature's voices evermore
    Keep singing through thy soul:

The wail of winds among the rocks,
    The laughter of the rills,
The silence of the dreary moors,
    The thunder of the hills!
Thy spirit was a cell wherein
    They lov'd to linger long,
And baptiz'd in its living font
    They started into song!

The bridegroom on his bridal day,
    Doats not upon his bride
With look of deeper love, than thou
    On our romantic Clyde.
Her Highland and her Lowland haunts,
    Are dear unto thy breast;
But dearer far, than each, than all—
    My green glens of the West!

And led by thee, once more we see
    The green haunts of the gowan;
Again we dream, beside the stream,
    Beneath the haw and rowan.

And lov'd ones that are now no more,
  From out their graves will start,
And wander with me as of yore,
  Upon the banks of Cart.

And how you lov'd to linger round
  The ruins old and hoar!
Where mighty chiefs and warriors dwelt,
  And minstrels sang of yore:
Old Crookston castle's mould'ring walls,
  And Stanley's turrets gray;
And hoary Garnock, telling tales
  Of glory past away.

And how you lov'd the ruin'd shrines,
  Where sits grey Melancholy,
Still calling to the passer-by—
  "Pause! for the place is holy!"
Is not "Gray Paisley's" Abbey hoar,
  An old world-weary moan,
A solemn chant! a holy hymn!
  A prayer that's breathed in stone!

And with what joy you hung around
  Our fields renown'd in story!
And how your eye burn'd in the light
  Of Scotland's ancient glory!
And with unwearied feet you traced
  Her scenes renown'd in song;
The streams that gush, and leap, and rush
  In deathless strains along.

And how you lov'd to treasure up
  The snatches of old rhymes,
Quaint epitaphs and legends old,
  The tales of other times.

And many a pilgrimage you made,
　　As if you fain would number
The moss-grown—the forgotten graves,
　　Where Scotia's martyrs slumber.

Thy feet shall tread those haunts no more,
　　And Spring with all her train,
Shall miss her pilgrim of the moor,
　　The mountain, and the plain.
Dear heart, farewell! we cannot tell
　　Where thou art laid to rest;
But, may the flowers you lov'd so well,
　　Aye bloom upon thy breast!

SIGHS IN THE CITY.

WEARILY my days are past;
For my heavy lot is cast
In the crowded city vast.

How my spirit longs to be
From this dreary prison free—
Oh, the laughing meads for me!

Oh! to follow the cuckoo,
While the glades are drapt wi' dew,
And the lark is in the blue!

Oh, to tread the flowery sod,
Free from all this heavy load—
One with Nature and with God!

Spring is forth with joyous air,
Strewing gems so rich and rare,
Showering gowans everywhere.

I will go where'er she goes,
Pausing often where she throws
The vi'let, and the red, red rose.

And we'll seek the glades of green,
Where the honeysuckles lean,
And the bluwarts ope their een;

Where the auld witch hazels hing,
And the woodbines creep and cling,
Round about the lonely spring;

Where the birds are blithe aboon,
And the laughing runnels rin
Onward in their merry din,

Treading paths the wild bee knows;
Where the grass the greenest grows,
In the haunts of the primrose.

Where the foxglove, fair and tall,
Leans against the rocky wall,
List'ning to the waterfall;

Where the bonnie hawthorn hings.
And the wee gray lintie sings
Of unutterable things:

And half hidden by the weeds,
Bonnie bluebells hing their heads,
Drapt wi' dew, like siller beads.

And the lily, meek and mild,
Blooming in the lonely wild,
That I lov'd so when a child!

Little wildlings, pure and bright,
Still, as to my childhood's sight,
Ye're a rapture, a delight!

Far from those who buy and sell,
I will seek the quiet dell—
Lonely ones with you to dwell!

Where no worldling soils the sod,
I'll live in your green abode.
One with Nature and with God.

WHEN GEORGE THE FOURTH WAS KING.

HOW green the braes were in the days
    When life was in its spring!
The heart was light, the world was bright,
    When George the Fourth was King!

Then buttercups and fairy haps
    Cam' laughing in wi' May;
And mirly birds wi' downy caps
    Were singing a' the day.

Then nature's bosom had a beat
    Which nothing could destroy;
The very grass beneath our feet
    Look'd up and laughed for joy.

Oh, then the sun had ne'er a spot;
    And all was green and gold;
And in our inmost hearts we thought
    We never would grow old,

But oh, the flowers have lost their hue!
    The birds they dinna sing
Sae sweetly as they used to do,
    When George the Fourth was King!

Then mirth in ilka cottage rang,
    For they were plenished weel;
And rosy lasses laughing sang
    Beside the spinning wheel.

And buskit in their hame-spun gray:
   But they were trig and braw,
Tho' ne'er a crinoline had they,
   They stole the heart awa'.

But fashion rules the world now,
   And oh, its heart is cold!
And love is no' the sacred lowe
   It was in days of old.

Oh! weary fa' this waefu' pride!
   It's banished rock and reel;
And joy has fled the country side,
   With Scotland's spinning wheel.

And weary fa' this waefu' lore
   Which only makes us vain;
The tree of knowledge as of yore,
   Has brought but grief and pain.

How green the braes were in the days
   When life was in its spring!
The heart was light, the world was bright,
   When George the Fourth was king!

THE AGE OF JOLLITY.

THE age, ah me! of jollity,
    Is number'd with the past;
For our new world, her lip has curl'd,
    And we've all grown good at last.

The joyous ways of our youthful days,
    No more in the land are known;
With the rock and reel, and the spinning wheel,
    They are gone, for ever gone!
And the Maypole gay, has passed away,
    And the dance upon the green—
And the Hogmanay, and the New-Year's-day,
    And the joyous Hallowe'en.

And the legends old, which then were told,
    And the fairy tales of yore;
With the minstrel's lay, ah, well-a-day!
    They are heard in the land no more.
And the fairs of old, with their joys untold,
    Which the young heart doated on;
With the puppet shows, and the dancing jo's,
    They are gone, for ever gone.

We've nae bairns noo, with the rose-red hue,
    That romp in the wood and glen;
But in their place we've got a race,
    Not o' weans, but o' wee, wee men—
Wha calculate, at nae sma' rate,
    And are always taking stock
For saving cash, all else is trash
    To our wonderfu' wee folk.

And what have we got, our sires had not,
    In our intellectual march,
Save vain conceit, and the way to cheat,
    With our stiff'ning and our starch?
Oh, give to me the spirit free,
    With the ringing laugh and roar;
And the simple heart, devoid of art,
    As it was in the days of yore.

    Lament with me, for jollity
      Is number'd with the past;
    For our prim world, her lip has curl'd,
      And we've all grown good at last.

OLD ADAM.

OLD ADAM was a character,
    Old Adam was a sage;
Ye'll hardly find his marrow now,
    In this degen'rate age.
He wore aboon his raven locks
    A braid kilmarnock bonnet,
A hamcart coat upon his back,
    Wi' big horn buttons on it.

A plaid out-owre his shouthers hung,
    The en' fell owre his sleeve;
A crooket, knotet, hazel rung
    Was in his wally nieve.
His breeks were side, sae were his shoon,
    His legs they were nae rashes,
And button'd upward to the knee,
    Wi' great drab splatterdashes !

A ringin' laugh, a hearty shake,
    A bright eye beaming o'er you ;
Ahint him Towser wags his tail,
    And there he stands before you !
And yet the inner man was form'd,
    On nature's model plan;
The dress but hid a heart that lov'd
    All Nature, God, and Man.

He was nae *thing* that stood apart
    Frae universal nature;
But had a corner in his heart
    For ev'ry living creature.

And after him, o'er a' the toon,
   The dogs delighted ran;
The very kitlins kent fu' well,
   He was nae common man.

His heart was just a living spring,
   Wi' sympathy o'erflowing;
And round its brim, the sweetest flowers,
   Of Love, and Hope, were blowing.
To see him—and to hear him speak—
   To look but in his face,
It made you fa' in love somehow,
   Wi' a' the human race.

A secret charm, a hidden spell,
   A mystery had bound him;
An atmosphere of calm delight,
   Was always hanging round him;
'Twas even in the dress he wore,
   For tho' his coat was cloutit,
Ye never saw't, or if ye saw,
   Ye thocht nae mair about it.

I ne'er could solve the mystery,
   By words that drappit frae him,
I felt, but couldna' find the way,
   He carried conquest wi' him.
And weel I lik'd to sit and read
   The language o' his e'e;
And try to sound the hidden deeps
   Of that untroubled sea.

The maist o' folk wha would be guid,
   And keep frae doing evil,
Maun aft hae battles wi' themselves,
   As weel as wi' the deevil.

And some are guid by grace o' God,
    And some hae to be skelpit;
But he was guid, and just because
    He wasna fit to help it.

His joy was in the woods to rove,
    To loiter by the burn;
He lov'd wild nature, and she lov'd
    Her lover in return.
He sought her green retired nooks,
    And nae ane better knew
The secret haunts, the fairy howes,
    Where a' the wild flowers grew.

And he would follow in the track
    Where spring had newly been,
To see the primrose peeping forth,
    And blewarts ope their e'en.
The gowan didna better lo'e
    Nor did the foxglove ken,
The hazel howes, the fairy knowes
    O' bonnie Calder glen.

Ilk strange wee bird o' wood and wild,
    'Bout which the learn'd disputit,
Its name, its nature, and its sang,—
    Weel kent he a' about it.
And when the wee gray lintie cam'
    Around his cot to sing,
He wadna let the vagrant touch
    A feather o' her wing.

And oh! how he would sing the sangs
    O' langsyne's happy days,
'Till we were wafted back again
    Amang the broomy braes.

We felt the magic o' the wood,
  As we were wont to do,
When we would hush our hearts to hear
  The voice o' the cuckoo.

Ance mair, the flowers were living things
  That round about us sprung;
It wasna' dew, but siller draps
  That on their bosoms hung!
The sky again was bonnie blue,
  Where no' a speck was seen;
And oh! the grass was green again—
  I canna tell how green.

We felt the breath o' meadows sweet,
  Ere yet the dews depart;
And ho! ance mair the gowan fair,
  Had crept into our heart.
And tho' he's lain him down to rest,
  Frae a' earth's good or ill;
His memory is fragrant yet—
  He's singing to us still.

THE HALLS OF HOLYROOD.

LET me sit as evening falls
 In sad and solemn mood,
Among the now deserted halls
 Of ancient Holyrood;
And think how human power and pride
 Must sink into decay,
Or like the bubbles on the tide,
   Pass, pass away.

No more the joyous crowd resorts
 To see the archers good,
Draw bow within the ringing courts
 Of merry Holyrood;
Ah, where's that high and haughty race
 That here so long held sway,
And where the phantoms they would chase?
   Passed, passed away!

And where the Monks and Friars gray,
 That oft in jovial mood,
Would revel till the break of day
 In merry Holyrood?
The flagons deep are emptied out,
 The revellers all away;
They come not to renew the bout—
   Where, where are they?

And where the plaided chieftains bold
    That round their monarch stood :
And where the damsels that of old
    Made merry Holyrood ?
And where that fair, ill-fated Queen,
    And where the minstrels gray,
That made those vaulted arches ring—
    Where, where are they ?

Though mould'ring are the minstrels' bones,
    Their thoughts have time withstood—
They live in snatches of old songs
    Of ancient Holyrood.
For thrones and dynasties depart,
    And diadems decay,
But these old gushings of the heart,
        Pass not away.

WE'RE A' JOHN TAMSON'S BAIRNS.

O, COME and listen to my sang,
   Nae matter wha ye be,
For there's a human sympathy
   That sings to you and me;
For as some kindly soul has said—
   All underneath the starns,
Despite of country, clime, and creed,
   Are a' John Tamson's bairns.

The higher that we clim' the tree,
   Mair sweert are we to fa',
And, spite o' fortune's heights and houghs,
   Death equal-aquals a';
And a' the great and mighty anes
   Wha slumber 'neath the cairns,
They ne'er forgot, though e'er so great,
   We're a' John Tamson's bairns.

Earth's heroes spring frae high and low,
   There's beauty in ilk place,
There's nae monopoly o' worth
   Amang the human race;
And genius ne'er was o' a class,
   But, like the moon and starns,
She sheds her kindly smile alike
   On a' John Tamson's bairns.

There's nae monopoly o' pride—
   For a' wi' Adam fell—
I've seen a joskin sae transformed,
   He scarcely kent himsel'.

The langer that the wise man lives,
　　The mair he sees and learns,
And aye the deeper care he takes
　　Owre a' John Tamson's bairns.

There's some distinction, ne'er a doubt,
　　'Tween Jock and Master John,
And yet its maistly in the dress,
　　When everything is known;
Where'er ye meet him, rich or poor,
　　The man o' sense and harns,
By moral worth he measures a'
　　Puir auld John Tamson's bairns.

There's ne'er been country yet nor kin
　　But has some weary flaw,
And he's the likest God aboon
　　Wha loves them ane and a';
And after a' that's come and gane,
　　What human heart but yearns,
To meet at last in licht and love,
　　Wi' a' John Tamson's bairns.

LONGINGS IN LONDON.

MY soul is sick of those miles of brick,
    I'm weary of " London Town ;"
I long to flee from this dismal sea,
    And to Scotland hurry down.
I'm weary of smoke, and pale faced folk,
    And I long to flee away;
I long to breathe on the mountain heath,
    As a school-boy longs for play.

I'm sick of routine, I would change the scene,
    O! give me the life that thrills;
Exchange dead books, for the living brooks,
    And the joy of the savage hills.
O! set me free, and away I'll flee
    With the live things of the rocks,
And be as of old, a hunter bold,
    In the land of herds and flocks.

O! for the joy without alloy
    'Mong the hills of Highland Dee,
Where torrents roar, and the eagles soar,
    And the stag is bounding free.
O! for the tent, on the heather bent,
    And the hardy Highland fare;
And the wild halloo of our jovial crew,
    In our short relief from care.

O! for the flock at rest by the rock,
    Each stag with his lordly crown;
How still they lie, 'neath the bending sky,
    And the great hills looking down.

O! for the dash, at the rifle's flash,
    While the wounded roe-buck strains,
And the bounding blood, like a roaring flood,
    Is sweeping through our veins.

As we take the track, with the yelling pack,
    And the startled hills reply—
Delirious joy! all earth's a toy
    When the chase lights up the eye!
O! respite rare, from the city's care,
    And its artificial pains,
With the pack to be on the mountains free,
    And the savage in our veins.

www.ingramcontent.com/pod-product-compliance
Lightning Source LLC
Chambersburg PA
CBHW021835230426
43669CB00008B/981